W9-BEC-833

SCOTT FORESMAN · ADDISON WESLEY

Mathematics

Grade 4

Enrichment Masters/Workbook

PEARSON

Scott
Foresman

Editorial Offices: Glenview, Illinois • Parsippany, New Jersey • New York, New York

Sales Offices: Parsippany, New Jersey • Duluth, Georgia • Glenview, Illinois
Coppell, Texas • Ontario, California • Mesa, Arizona

Overview

Enrichment Masters/Workbook enhances student learning by actively involving students in different areas of mathematical reasoning. Activities often involve students in real-world situations, some of which may have more than one right answer. Thus, the masters motivate students to find alternate solutions to a given problem.

How to use

The *Enrichment Masters/Workbook* is designed so that the teacher can use it in many different ways.

- As a teaching tool to guide students in exploring a specific type of thinking skill. Making a transparency of the worksheet provides an excellent way to expedite this process as students work at their desks along with the teacher.

- As an enrichment worksheet that challenges and motivates students to hone their thinking skills.

- As independent or group work.

- As a homework assignment that encourages students to involve their parents in the educational process.

ISBN 0-328-04935-2

Copyright © Pearson Education, Inc.

All Rights Reserved. Printed in the United States of America. This publication, or parts thereof, may be used with appropriate equipment to reproduce copies for classroom use only.

17 18 19 20 V084 14 13 12 11 10

Table of Contents

Table of Contents continued

Changing Places

Look at the chart. Something has happened to the place value of each starting number. Write the part that is missing in each row. Use the sample to help you.

Starting Number	Change Place	Ending Number
1,426	2 tens *less*	1,406
1. 73,458	3 thousands *more*	
2.	5 ones *less*	496,350
3. 91,858		91,758
4. 8,537	6 tens *more*	
5.	4 hundred thousands *more*	754,311
6. 172,618		102,618
7. 342		9,342
8.	1 ten *less*	254,008
9. 121,021	11 tens *more*	
10. 594,637	1 ten thousand *more*	
11.	3 thousands *less*	723,432
12. 99,999		100,009

© Pearson Education, Inc. 4

Puzzling Place Values

Write the missing number or word in each blank to complete each sentence.

1. Thirty million, three has _____ digits.

2. You need _____ digits to make a number that is 1 less than 100,000,000.

3. The value of the 7 in 427,208,311 is _____.

4. The number two million, four hundred one thousand, two has _____ digits.

5. The digits in sixty-five million, three hundred eighty-one thousand, two hundred four have a sum of _____.

6. Five hundred twenty-four million, two hundred eighty thousand, four hundred has a _____ in the ten millions place.

7. The number that is 2 more than 99,999,999 has _____ zeros.

8. In the number 304,248,168, there is a 4 in the _____ place and in the _____ place.

9. The number _____ is fifty thousand more than 15,343,014.

10. Twenty-five thousand nine hundred eighty-one is _____ less than 25,984.

2 Use with Lesson 1-2.

© Pearson Education, Inc. 4

Letter Codes

Each letter in the nine-letter words below has been given a digit. Each word represents a different place value. Jellyfish represents the ten-thousands digits, porcupine represents the thousands, crocodile represents the hundreds, angelfish represents the tens, and bumblebee represents the ones.

Ten thousands

J	E	L	L	Y	F	I	S	H
1	2	3	4	5	6	7	8	9

Thousands

P	O	R	C	U	P	I	N	E
1	2	3	4	5	6	7	8	9

Hundreds

C	R	O	C	O	D	I	L	E
1	2	3	4	5	6	7	8	9

Tens

A	N	G	E	L	F	I	S	H
1	2	3	4	5	6	7	8	9

Ones

B	U	M	B	L	E	B	E	E
1	2	3	4	5	6	7	8	9

Use the code to find the words that the numbers represent.

1. 4,217

_____

2. 1,729

_____

3. 213

_____

4. 92,286

_____

5. 3,388

_____

6. 86,729

_____

© Pearson Education, Inc. 4

Chart-Topping Rivers

The names of some of the world's longest rivers are in the table. Count how many of the five vowels each river name has. Tally those findings in the chart below. Answer the questions that follow using the information you found.

River	Country
Amazon	Brazil
Nile	Egypt
Mississippi	U.S.
Chang	China
Yenisey	Russia

	A	E	I	O	U
Amazon	II			I	
Nile					
Mississippi					
Chang					
Yenisey					
TOTAL					

1. Which rivers contain both an E and an I?

_____

2. Which rivers contain at least one A?

_____

3. Which vowel is used the most in the river names?

_____

4. Which vowel is not used in the river names?

_____

5. How many more times are E and I used in the names than A and O?

_____

© Pearson Education, Inc. 4

Follow the Leader

Find the path to the finish line. You may only travel to a greater number. You may not move diagonally. Color the boxes as you find your way.

Start

1	0	3	17,642	7	1,543	1,727	1,848	18,603
7	10	9	183	1,572	1,600	1,847	1,849	3,722
6	26	15	205	206	955	842	763	7,026
31	49	37	207	444	701	83	8,303	8,103
62	73	112	150	35	697	98	9,265	8,100
17	59	97	3	9,621	14	19,423	15,211	12,964
12,043	703	84	12,652	30,654	7,342	19,464	1,643	1,673
1,334	945	3	7,003	632	948	21,190	23,023	25,901

Finish

© Pearson Education, Inc. 4

Quick Math

The students in Mrs. Barnwell's science class learned a lot about the speed of different animals.

A crocodile can run about 10 km per hour.

1. Find and circle the speeds of a crocodile that round to 10.

16   4   17   8   6   12

A red deer can run about 80 km per hour.

2. Find and circle the speeds of a red deer that round to 80.

67   78   82   85   90   76

An elephant is very large, but it can run about 40 km per hour!

3. Find and circle the speeds of an elephant that round to 40.

41   44   52   36   49   38

A cheetah can run about 110 km per hour.

4. Find and circle the speeds of a cheetah that round to 110.

114   124   115   108   118   105

An ostrich can run about 50 km per hour.

5. Find and circle the speeds of an ostrich that round to 50.

41   52   47   54   46   59

A hare can run about 70 km per hour.

6. Find and circle the speeds of a hare that round to 70.

74   64   67   71   79   69

© Pearson Education, Inc. 4

About One Million

Circle the best estimate for each question. Then, explain how you could check your answer.

1. If one book is about 10 in. high, about how many books would be in a stack that is 1,000,000 in. high?

   A. 1 million books   **B.** 5 million books   **C.** 100 thousand books

   _____

   _____

2. If 1 million people visited the zoo this year, about how many people visited every week? (Remember: There are 52 weeks in 1 year.)

   A. 20,000 people   **B.** 10,000 people   **C.** 2,000 people

   _____

   _____

3. If there are about 30 days in each month, about how many months are in 1 million days?

   A. 40,000 months   **B.** 30,000 months   **C.** 20,000 months

   _____

   _____

4. About how many years would it take to give away 1 million dollars if you give away 1 dollar every minute?

   A. 2 years   **B.** 5 years   **C.** 10 years

   _____

   _____

© Pearson Education, Inc. 4

Aquarium Time

Aquarium Tour Schedule

Introduction: Aquarium history 🐟
Part 1:   Freshwater fish 🐟 🐟 🐟
Part 2:   Saltwater fish 🐟 🐟 🐟 🐟
Part 3:   Penguins and sea lions 🐟 🐟 🐟 🐟
Part 4:   Sharks 🐟 🐟
Part 5:   Dolphin show 🐟 🐟 🐟 🐟 🐟 🐟
Closing: Questions and answers 🐟 🐟 🐟

🐟 = 5 minutes

Tours begin every hour from 9 A.M. to 4 P.M.

1. How long does the dolphin show last?

_____

2. How long does the entire tour last?

_____

3. Which parts of the tour last longer than the Closing?

_____

4. Which parts of the tour are shorter than Part 3?

_____

_____

5. Marvin began his tour at 10:00 A.M. What time will his tour end?

_____

6. Pam began her tour at 1:00 P.M. She plans to meet her friends at 2:40 P.M. Will the tour end in time?

_____

© Pearson Education, Inc. 4

Similar Shapes

Look at the group of shapes on the left and find something that
all of the shapes in the group have in common. Then, circle the
shape on the right that belongs in the group.

1.

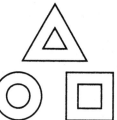

2.

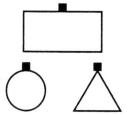

3.

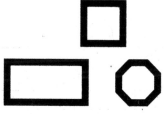

4.

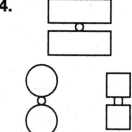

© Pearson Education, Inc. 4

Name_____

Toy Store

Sam is counting up the money he has saved to buy some toys at the store. Help him count the following amounts and decide which toys he could buy with each amount.

Toys	
Top	$1.00
Car	$1.75
Ball	$2.00
Bear	$4.50
Book	$4.25
Doll	$8.40
Puzzle	$4.00

1. 4 quarters, 1 dime, 3 nickels, 2 pennies

_____

_____

_____

2. Two $5 bills, 1 dollar, 3 quarters, 6 dimes, 1 nickel, 5 pennies

_____

_____

3. Sam pays the exact amount for one item. He gives the clerk 1 dollar, 1 quarter, 7 dimes, and 5 pennies. Which item did he buy?

_____

4. Sam buys 2 toys. He gives the clerk one $5 bill, 2 dollars, 5 quarters, 3 dimes, and 4 nickels. He does not get any change. Which 2 toys did Sam buy?

_____

5. What coins did Sam use to buy the car if he gave the clerk 1 dollar and 11 coins?

_____

_____

© Pearson Education, Inc. 4

Name_____

Vacation Computation

Read each story. Then find and circle all of the answers that could be true. There may be more than one correct answer.

1. The Pak family wants to go to Miami, Florida, for a vacation. They found a hotel for 5 days that costs $89 per night. Which of the following answers could be true?

   A. They will get change back if they pay with $500.

   B. They do not have enough money if they pay with $500.

   C. If they pay with $500, they could stay one extra night.

2. The Paks decide to drive from Chicago, Illinois, to Miami. They will drive on many roads as they travel the total of 1,379 mi. The three main roads they travel are Interstate-65 for 433 mi, Interstate-24 for 141 mi, and Interstate-75 for 480 mi. Which of the following answers could be true?

   A. The total miles on the three main roads are most of the miles they will travel.

   B. They will only travel on three roads.

   C. They will travel about 300 mi on the other roads.

3. The total time driving to Miami will be 22 hr and 11 min. Which of the following answers could be true?

   A. If they drive without stopping, it will take two days to get there.

   B. If Mr. Pak and Mrs. Pak each drive for half of the time, they will each drive about 11 hr.

   C. If the Paks start driving at 8:00 A.M. and drive without stopping, they will arrive in Miami the next morning.

© Pearson Education, Inc. 4

Name_____

Decimal Patterns

Write the next two numbers in each pattern.

1. 0.2, 0.4, 0.6, _____, _____

2. thirty-three hundredths, thirty-four hundredths, thirty-five hundredths,

_____, _____

3. 1.7, 1.8, 1.9, _____, _____

4. fourteen hundredths, sixteen hundredths, eighteen hundredths,

_____, _____

5. 1.27, 1.24, 1.21, 1.18, 1.15, _____, _____

6. two tenths, twenty hundredths, three tenths, thirty hundredths, four tenths,

_____, _____

7. 1.45, 1.4, 1.35, 1.3, 1.25, _____, _____

8. three tenths, six tenths, nine tenths, one and two tenths, one and five tenths,

_____, _____

9. five tenths, forty-five hundredths, four tenths, thirty-five hundredths, three tenths,

_____, _____

10. 2.2, 2.0, 1.8, 1.6, 1.4, _____, _____

11. 0.09, 0.14, 0.19, 0.24, 0.29, _____, _____

12. thirty-seven hundredths, thirty-three hundredths, twenty-nine hundredths, twenty-five hundredths, twenty-one hundredths,

_____, _____

© Pearson Education, Inc. 4

Number Mazes

Follow the rules to find your way through the mazes.

1. You can only enter a square with a number whose digits add up to a sum that is greater than 30.

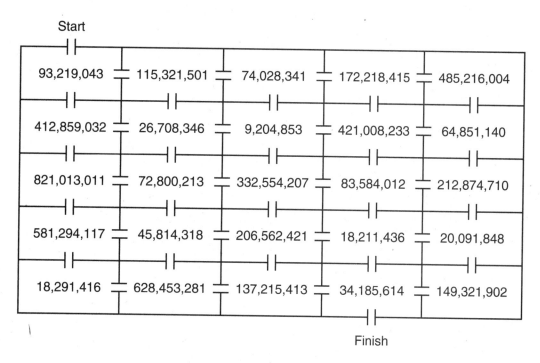

Start

93,219,043	115,321,501	74,028,341	172,218,415	485,216,004
412,859,032	26,708,346	9,204,853	421,008,233	64,851,140
821,013,011	72,800,213	332,554,207	83,584,012	212,874,710
581,294,117	45,814,318	206,562,421	18,211,436	20,091,848
18,291,416	628,453,281	137,215,413	34,185,614	149,321,902

Finish

2. You can only enter a square that has a digit in the ten-millions place that has a greater value than the ten-millions digit in the number in the square you moved from.

Start

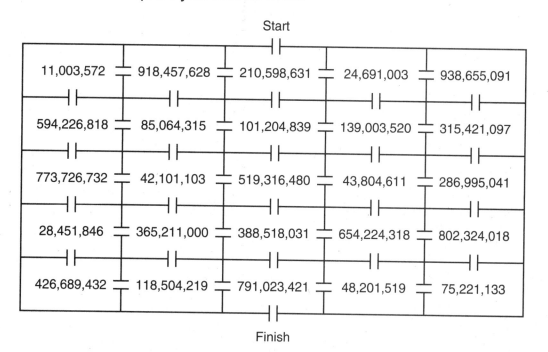

11,003,572	918,457,628	210,598,631	24,691,003	938,655,091
594,226,818	85,064,315	101,204,839	139,003,520	315,421,097
773,726,732	42,101,103	519,316,480	43,804,611	286,995,041
28,451,846	365,211,000	388,518,031	654,224,318	802,324,018
426,689,432	118,504,219	791,023,421	48,201,519	75,221,133

Finish

© Pearson Education, Inc. 4

Name_____

Student Plays

Marta's class is working in groups of 7 students to present plays to the class. Use the comments made by the students in Marta's group to decide who will be responsible for each position.

Marta: "I do not want to design the set or the costumes."

Calvin: "I like sewing and designing clothing, but I can also direct."

Andrew: "I enjoy writing and playing music."

Louisa: "I am good at organizing and directing people."

Diego: "I enjoy speaking in front of the class."

Jackie: "I will do anything except direct the play."

Helen: "I am interested in painting and designing, but I do not like to sew."

1. Directing the play _____.

2. Designing the set _____.

3. Designing and sewing the costumes _____.

4. Playing the music _____.

5. Acting in the play (Hint: There will be three students acting in the play.)

_____

6. If your first choice for director was unable to participate, whom would you choose as a replacement? Explain.

_____

_____

_____

© Pearson Education, Inc. 4

Mental Puzzles

Using mental math to add helps you find tens and hundreds.

1. Look at each number in the puzzle board. Find two numbers in the box whose sum equals that number. Use each number *only once*. Do not use paper and pencil or a calculator.

119	225	511	259	173	28
486	374	375	227	164	314
389	136	72	241	81	326

Puzzle Board		
100 + ____ ____	200 + ____ ____	300 + ____ ____
400 + ____ ____	500 + ____ ____	600 + ____ ____
700 + ____ ____	800 + ____ ____	900 + ____ ____

2. Explain what methods you used to help you solve the puzzle board.

_____

_____

_____

_____

© Pearson Education, Inc. 4

Name_____

Matching Shapes

E 2-2
VISUAL THINKING

These two shapes are the same.
The second shape is turned.

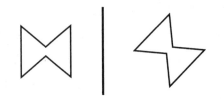

Match each turned shape.

1. |

2. |

3.  |

4. |

5.  |

16 Use with Lesson 2-2.

Canyon Trip

You are going on a three-day camping trip in the Grand Canyon. The chart shows the weights of some equipment you may need. Each person must take at least 2 water canteens and 3 food tins on the trip.

Equipment	Weight (lb)
Water canteen	1
Food tin	2
Compass	1
Shovel	5
Binoculars	3
Tent	8
Chair	10
Pillow	2
Extra clothes	7
Cooking pots/pans	30
Sleeping cushion	4

1. You are going to hike alone and carry a backpack. The backpack can hold up to 25 lb. What equipment will you take on the trip?

   _____

   _____

   _____

   _____

2. You are hiking with 2 friends. Each will carry 1 backpack. The 3 of you can carry up to 75 lb. You will only need 1 tent. What equipment will you take on the trip?

   _____

   _____

   _____

3. You and 4 friends are taking donkeys on the trip. The donkeys can carry 180 lb. You will not take backpacks. You will need 2 tents. What equipment will you take on the trip?

   _____

   _____

   _____

   _____

© Pearson Education, Inc. 4

Charming Necklaces

Jacklyn makes charm necklaces. She needs to make 10 necklaces like the one shown below.

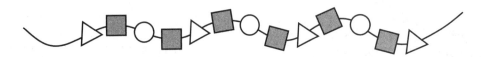

Jacklyn has the following choices of charms to purchase to make her necklaces.

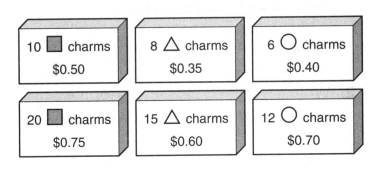

| 10 ▪ charms $0.50 | 8 △ charms $0.35 | 6 ◯ charms $0.40 |
| 20 ▪ charms $0.75 | 15 △ charms $0.60 | 12 ◯ charms $0.70 |

1. How many of each charm will Jacklyn need to make 10 necklaces?

_____

_____

2. How many packages of square charms will Jacklyn need to buy if she buys the 10-charm packages?

_____

3. How much will Jacklyn pay if she buys all of the triangle charms she needs in 15-charm packages?

_____

4. Explain one way Jacklyn could buy the number of each kind of charm she needs for the necklaces. How much will it cost?

_____

_____

_____

_____

© Pearson Education, Inc. 4

Spaghetti Dinner

A community center is holding a spaghetti dinner to raise
$700 for a new playground. You are in charge of the budget.
The expenses are shown below.

Expenses	
Item	**Amount**
Spaghetti	$ 80
Tomato sauce	$130
Juice	$ 75
Tablecloths	$ 68
Plates and utensils	$ 54
Napkins	$ 23
Garlic bread	$ 96
Renting the hall	$200

1. The center already has $150 saved
   for the playground. How much
   more does the center need?

   _____

2. What are the total expenses for the
   dinner?

   _____

3. How much money does the community center need to
   raise to pay the expenses and have enough money
   for the playground?   _____

4. Sam was able to buy garlic bread from a bakery
   for $52. By how much did this lower the budget?   _____

5. You expect 200 people to attend the dinner. Gloria says if
   people pay $6 each, the center will make enough money
   for the playground. Do you agree? If not, explain and
   suggest a different price per person.

   _____

   _____

   _____

   _____

   _____

   _____

© Pearson Education, Inc. 4

Name _____

Use Your Head

Look at the problem and the answer. Without actually adding the problem, decide whether or not the given answer is reasonable. Write *Yes* or *No* and explain your answer.

1.
```
   224
   303
+  125
   652
```

2.
```
   300
   478
+  213
   991
```

_____

_____

_____

_____

_____

_____

3.
```
   24
   56
+  15
   83
```

4.
```
   18,207
    4,956
+   2,345
  101,217
```

_____

_____

_____

_____

_____

_____

5.
```
 $310.58
  207.90
+ 189.03
 $707.51
```

6.
```
   2,341
   4,750
+  1,532
  80,623
```

_____

_____

_____

_____

_____

_____

© Pearson Education, Inc. 4

Name_____

Park Conclusions

Each person made a conclusion about the data in the table.
Think about each person's conclusion. Do you agree? Explain.

Protected National Parks

Country	Number of Parks	Total Size (km^2)
Canada	237	309,529
United States	59	202,320
Japan	15	12,991
Australia	339	275,551
New Zealand	11	21,011
Finland	17	3,541
France	5	2,613

1. Kylie compared the number of square kilometers of protected park land in the United States and Canada. She concluded that Canada has 97,209 km^2 more protected park land than the United States.

_____

_____

2. Franklin looked at the number of protected national parks in the United States and Australia. He concluded that Australia has 280 more protected parks than the United States.

_____

_____

3. Theona concluded that Canada has 130 more protected parks than the United States, Japan, New Zealand, Finland, and France altogether.

_____

_____

© Pearson Education, Inc. 4

Name_____

So Many Decisions!

The local sports store is holding an anniversary sale. As part of the sale, every 100th customer gets a chance to win prizes. Each selected shopper gets 15 min to fill a shopping cart with sporting goods and clothing. If the total price of the items is more than $280 but less than $300, the shopper keeps everything in the cart.

Here is a list of sporting goods and clothing. Place a check mark next to any item you would put in the cart. Then find your total.

Item	Price	Item	Price
____ Baseball	$ 4.99	____ Bicycle	$178.99
____ Football	$17.95	____ Tennis racket	$ 29.79
____ Basketball	$21.99	____ Tennis balls	$ 7.25
____ Hockey puck	$ 8.50	____ Sweatshirt	$ 16.99
____ Baseball glove	$34.99	____ Shoes	$ 41.50
____ Running shorts	$11.50	____ Weight set	$ 89.99
____ Cycling gloves	$16.00	____ In-line skates	$ 53.69
____ Stopwatch	$ 3.49	____ Gym ball	$ 1.99
____ Football helmet	$60.00	____ Baseball bat	$ 27.99
____ Golf clubs	$99.99	____ Golf balls	$ 14.50

1. What is your total price?

_____

2. Did you win your items?

_____

3. How did you decide which items to choose?

_____

_____

_____

_____

© Pearson Education, Inc. 4

Name_____

Where Do You Live?

Read the clues to find where each person lives in the apartment building. As you discover where each person lives, write the person's name in the apartment.

1. At Rosebud Terrace, there are 8 apartments. The names of the tenants are Bill, Madeline, Warrick, Pamela, Quincy, Salma, Todd, and Kendra.

   - Salma lives on the second floor.

   - Quincy lives directly above Warrick.

   - Bill lives next to Pamela.

   - Madeline lives to the left of Warrick and to the right of Kendra.

   - Todd lives to the left of Quincy.

   - Pamela lives right above Todd.

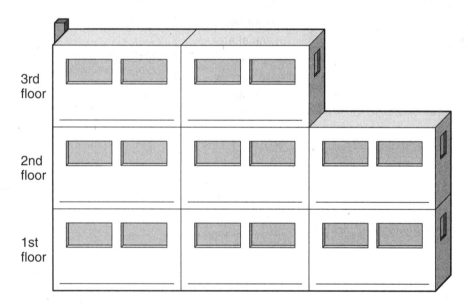

2. Explain how you found each person's place in the apartment building.

_____

_____

_____

© Pearson Education, Inc. 4

Name_____

Birdhouses

Cecilia owns a store that specializes in selling decorated birdhouses. The table at the right shows the number of birdhouses Cecilia sold each month. Write an expression to represent the following situations.

1. How many birdhouses did Cecilia sell in May and June together?

_____

2. How many more birdhouses did Cecilia sell in October than in September?

_____

3. What is the total number of birdhouses Cecilia sold from February through May?

_____

4. If Cecilia sold 152 birdhouses in May, how many birdhouses did she sell in January and May combined?

_____

5. If Cecilia sold 257 birdhouses in September, how many more birdhouses did she sell in September than in August?

_____

6. The company that makes the birdhouses is now charging $4 more for each birdhouse. If Cecilia used to pay b for each birdhouse, how much will she need to pay now?

_____

Birdhouses Sold

January	417
February	379
March	341
April	262
May	m
June	89
July	76
August	94
September	s
October	296
November	439
December	611

© Pearson Education, Inc. 4

Flying High

	Atlanta	Boston	Chicago	Dallas	Denver
Boston	946				
Chicago	606	867			
Dallas	721	1,555	796		
Denver	1,208	1,767	901	654	
Detroit	505	632	235	982	1,135

Use the air distance chart above to write a number sentence for each problem. Then solve.

1. How many more miles does it take to get from Denver to Atlanta than to get from Detroit to Atlanta and Chicago to Atlanta combined?

_____

2. Jorge flew from Dallas to Detroit, from Detroit to Denver, and from Denver back to Dallas. How many miles did Jorge fly altogether?

_____

3. Maria flew from her home city of Boston to Atlanta, back home to Boston, and then back to Atlanta. How many miles did she fly altogether?

_____

4. How many more miles is it to fly round-trip between Dallas and Boston than between Denver and Chicago?

_____

_____

© Pearson Education, Inc. 4

Break the Codes

The symbols in each set of problems represent whole numbers.
Break the codes.

Hint: Here's how you might break one code.

@ + ▲ = 27	Think: @ + @ = 24 is a double.
@ + @ = 24	The two addends are the same, so @ = 12.
	Since 27 − 12 = 15, ▲ = 15.

1.

$$\text{§} + \odot = 11$$

$$\text{§} - \odot = 1$$

$$\text{§} = \underline{\quad}, \odot = \underline{\quad}$$

2.

$$\star + \lozenge = 14$$

$$\lozenge + \lozenge + \lozenge = 12$$

$$\star = \underline{\quad}, \lozenge = \underline{\quad}$$

3.

$$\Leftleftarrow - \curlyvee = 9$$

$$\curlyvee + \Leftleftarrow = 17$$

$$\Leftleftarrow = \underline{\quad}, \curlyvee = \underline{\quad}$$

4.

$$\oslash + \boxtimes = 28$$

$$\boxtimes + \boxtimes = 16$$

$$\oslash = \underline{\quad}, \boxtimes = \underline{\quad}$$

5.

$$\hexagon + \wedge\!\wedge = 9$$

$$\wedge\!\wedge + \wedge\!\wedge = \hexagon$$

$$\hexagon = \underline{\quad}, \wedge\!\wedge = \underline{\quad}$$

6.

$$\triangle\!\triangle + \sim = \triangle\!\triangle$$

$$\triangle\!\triangle - \sim = 7$$

$$\triangle\!\triangle = \underline{\quad}, \sim = \underline{\quad}$$

7.

$$\text{cylinder} + 9 = \text{cube}$$

$$\text{cube} - \text{cylinder} = 9$$

$$1 + \text{cube} = 12$$

$$\text{cylinder} = \underline{\quad}, \text{cube} = \underline{\quad}$$

8.

$$\text{Y} + \text{V} + \triangle = 16$$

$$\text{Y} - \triangle = \triangle$$

$$\triangle + \triangle = 8$$

$$\text{Y} = \underline{\quad}, \text{V} = \underline{\quad}, \triangle = \underline{\quad}$$

© Pearson Education, Inc. 4

Algebra Cadabra!

Find the value for *x* in the following exercises.

1. $x + 7 + x = 15$ _____

2. $6 + 8 - x = 11$ _____

3. $6 + x + 6 = 15$ _____

4. $23 - 7 - x = 9$ _____

5. $10 + 4 + x = 22$ _____

6. $25 - x - x = 15$ _____

7. $12 + 24 - x - x - x = 18$ _____

8. $x + 5 + x + 4 = 27$ _____

9. $x + x + x - 4 - 3 - 2 = 12$ _____

10. $14 + x - 11 - x + x - 3 = 1$ _____

11. $29 + 31 + 40 - x - x - x - x - x = 0$ _____

12. $x + x + x + 6 + x + 4 + x + 9 + x = 67$ _____

13. $9 - 1 + x + 4 + x + x - 5 + x + x + x = 61$ _____

14. $x - 5 + x - 8 + x + x + 3 + 12 + 10 + x + x = 72$ _____

15. $46 - 3 + x + x + x + x + x + x + x - 15 = 42$ _____

© Pearson Education, Inc. 4

Name _____

Spread That Peanut Butter

The U.S. government requires all food products to show nutrition facts on the product label.

1. Four servings of peanut butter contain about 64 g of fat. Three servings contain about 48 g of fat. Use mental math to find the difference in fat between 3 and 4 servings of peanut butter. Explain your answer.

_____

_____

2. There are 200 calories in a serving of peanut butter. The number of calories from fat can be found by subtracting 60 from c, where c = the total number of calories. Find the number of calories from fat if $c = 200$.

_____

3. In two servings of peanut butter there are 14 g of carbohydrates. In 3 servings there are 21 g and in 5 servings there are 35 g. Find the pattern for the number of carbohydrates in n servings of peanut butter.

_____

_____

_____

Suppose that the price for a case of 24 jars of peanut butter is $57.36.

4. If the sale price for a case of peanut butter was $12.99 off the normal price, what would the sale price for 1 case be?

_____

5. If you spent $72.53 on groceries, and $9.56 was spent on peanut butter, how much did you spend on other groceries?

_____

© Pearson Education, Inc. 4

Hurray Array!

You can demonstrate multiplication by showing objects in an array.
There are two ways to set up an array with two factors.

For each array given, create a different array that shows the same
factors. Then write the multiplication sentence for each picture.

1. ○ ○ ○ ○ ○ ○
   ○ ○ ○ ○ ○ ○
   ○ ○ ○ ○ ○ ○ =   _____
   ○ ○ ○ ○ ○ ○

                     _____

2. □ □ □ □ □ □
   □ □ □ □ □ □ =   _____
   □ □ □ □ □ □

                     _____

There are at least two arrays for any product: the product × 1
and 1 × the product. Sometimes there are other possible arrays
for a product.

3. Draw the other array for the product 25.
   Write the multiplication sentence.   _____

4. Draw the other array for the product 9.
   Write the multiplication sentence.   _____

Sometimes there are several different arrays that can be drawn for a product.

5. Draw an array for the product 28 that is not 28 × 1, 1 × 28,
   7 × 4, or 4 × 7. Write the multiplication sentence for your array.

   _____

© Pearson Education, Inc. 4

Patterns, Patterns Everywhere

Complete each pattern and write the rule for the pattern you find. Hint: The pattern may involve more than one operation. For example, the numbers 2, 4, 16, 32, 128 form a pattern of multiplying by 2, then multiplying by 4.

Pattern Rule

1. 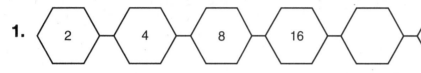 2 4 8 16 _____

2. 5 10 50 100 500 _____

3. 1 9 9 81 81 _____

4. 7 0 0 0 _____

5. 5 5 25 25 125 _____

6. 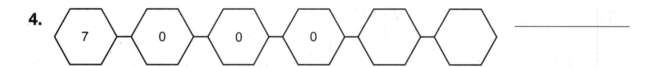 1 1 2 6 24 _____

7. Although a single starfish may have as many as 44 arms, we are most familiar with starfish that have 5 arms. Write a number pattern for 6 starfish if each had 5 arms. How many arms would those starfish have in all?

_____

_____

© Pearson Education, Inc. 4

Name_____

How Does Your Garden Grow?

Area is the name for the number of square units that are in a given space. You can figure out the area of a rectangle as you would an array. You can also break apart a rectangle to form different combinations and still have the same area.

Here is Mary's garden: $4 \times 6 = 24$ square units.

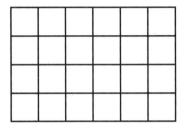

Draw lines and write the first letter of the flower to show several possible planting plans.

1.

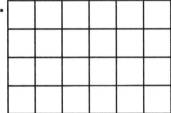

2×6 = tulips
2×4 = roses
2×2 = marigolds

2.

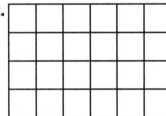

4×4 = tulips
2×2 = roses
2×2 = marigolds

3.

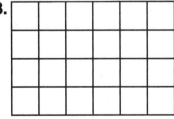

3×4 = tulips
1×6 = roses
3×2 = marigolds

4.

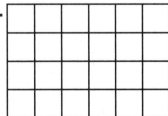

4×5 = tulips
1×3 = roses
1×1 = marigolds

© Pearson Education, Inc. 4

Name_____

Cube Turning

A lettered cube has 6 sides with a different letter on each side.
Each letter can be shown in 4 different positions.

1. How many different ways can the cube be displayed?

_____

Fill in the missing letters in the position they would be seen on
the cube. The first one has been done for you as an example.

Example:

2.

3.

4.

5.

6.

© Pearson Education, Inc. 4

Name_____

Recycling Numbers

Miles and Cynthia participated in a weeklong recycling project. Cynthia collected 4 cans every day, and Miles collected 3 cans every day.

1. Fill in the table to show how many cans each student has collected by the end of each day.

Days	1	2	3	4	5	6	7
Miles	3	6					
Cynthia	4	8					

2. At the end of the week, how many cans did Cynthia collect?

_____

3. At the end of the week, how many cans did Miles collect?

_____

4. If the pattern had continued for another week, a total of 14 days, how many cans would Cynthia have collected? How many would Miles have collected?

_____

5. The project was such a success, it was continued for 30 days. Complete the bar graph to compare the total cans collected by Miles and Cynthia.

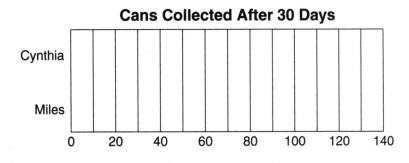

Cans Collected After 30 Days

© Pearson Education, Inc. 4

Baby-Sitting in the Neighborhood

Jennifer baby-sits for some of the families in her neighborhood. She wants to decide how she can earn the most money. She has made a chart that shows how long she usually baby-sits for a family and how much she is paid for her job.

Family	Hours	Amount Paid
Roberts	6	$30
Robinsons	6	$24
San Giacomos	8	$40
Lings	5	$35
Oberlins	7	$42

1. Which family pays the most per hour? What is the hourly rate?

_____

2. Which family pays the least per hour?

_____

3. Which would pay more, 8 hr of baby-sitting for the Oberlins or 7 hr of baby-sitting for the San Giacomos?

_____

_____

4. On one Friday night, Jennifer is asked to baby-sit for two different families. The Robinsons need her for 5 hr, and the Lings want her to baby-sit for 4 hr. If Jennifer can only take one job and wants to make the most money, which job should she take? How much will she earn?

_____

5. On a different Friday night, the Roberts offer Jennifer a 5-hour baby-sitting job with a $4 tip, and the Robinsons offer Jennifer an 8-hour baby-sitting job. Which job should Jennifer take? How much more will she earn?

_____

© Pearson Education, Inc. 4

Just the Fact(or)s

Some numbers have several factors. Complete the following
to find all of the factors of 12. The first one is done for you.

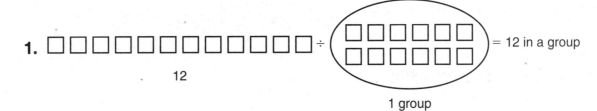

1. = 12 in a group
   12
   1 group

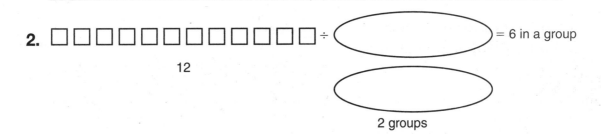

2. = 6 in a group
   12
   2 groups

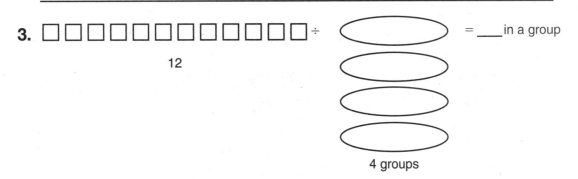

3. = ___ in a group
   12
   4 groups

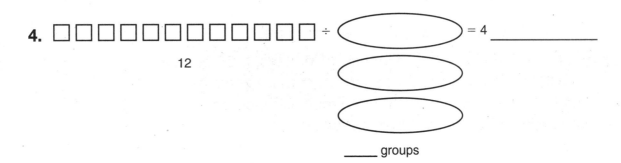

4. = 4 _____
   12
   ____ groups

5. There are 6 numbers that are factors of 12. What are they?

_____

© Pearson Education, Inc. 4

Divide and Conquer

Find the unknown value in the multiplication fact to help you complete the division fact. Write out both completed facts.

1. $6 \times m = 36 \quad \frac{36}{6} = m$

_____

2. $4 \times y = 28 \quad \frac{28}{y} = 4$

_____

3. $z \times 8 = 16 \quad \frac{16}{8} = z$

_____

4. $7 \times 8 = q \quad \frac{q}{8} = 7$

_____

5. $9 \times r = 54 \quad \frac{54}{r} = 9$

_____

6. $10 \times s = 10 \quad \frac{10}{10} = s$

_____

7. In a soccer match, each team has 11 players. If 24 people are willing to play a game of soccer, are there enough players for two full teams? Write a multiplication and division sentence to show your answer.

_____

_____

_____

© Pearson Education, Inc. 4

Analyze This

An analogy is often used to show the relationship between pairs of items.

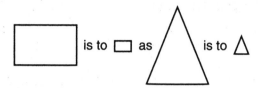

1. How are the drawings of the rectangles related?

_____

_____

2. How are the drawings of the triangles related?

_____

_____

3. Draw the missing item in the following analogies.

A.

B.

C.

D.

© Pearson Education, Inc. 4

Score More

Use the drawings to help you answer the questions.

1. You threw 3 darts. Each one hit the target.
   What is the greatest score you could get?
   What is the lowest?

   _____

Write number sentences that show your answer.

2. You threw 4 darts and your total was 23.
   What sections did you hit?

   _____

3. Could you hit another combination of 4 darts and score 23?

   _____

4. Could a challenger throw 4 darts, hit only one 9 and score
   higher than you?

   _____

5. You pushed 4 disks and scored 32
   points on this shuffleboard court. One
   disk was out of bounds. On which parts
   of the board did your disks land?

   _____

   _____

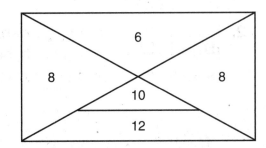

6. If you pushed 4 disks and all of them landed, show two
   ways you could score 34 points.

   _____

   _____

© Pearson Education, Inc. 4

Name_____

Graphing Sales

Fran grows vegetables in her garden, and then she sells them at
the market. A diagram of Fran's vegetable patch and a price list
for her vegetables are shown below.

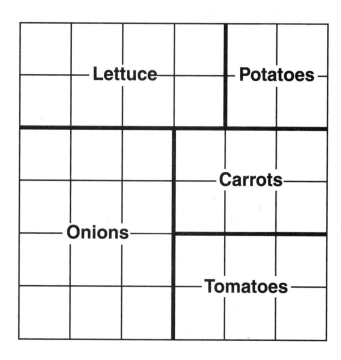

Fran's Fresh Produce		
Carrots	2 lb	$1
Onions	3 lb	$2
Tomatoes	3 lb	$5
Potatoes	2 lb	$3
Lettuce	1 lb	$2

1. How many squares are in Fran's garden?

_____

2. Each square in Fran's garden yields 2 lb of vegetables. If
   Fran plants every square in her garden, how many pounds
   of vegetables will she be able to grow?

_____

3. Fran makes $18 selling onions at the market. How many
   pounds of onions did she sell?

_____

4. A customer buys 6 lb of tomatoes, 4 lb of potatoes, and
   4 lb of carrots. He pays with a $50 bill. How much change
   should he get back?

_____

© Pearson Education, Inc. 4

Very Variable

1. A $1 bill represents 100 cents. The value of a dollar could also be represented by dimes. Divide the picture of the dollar to represent dimes. Complete the expression for the number of dimes in 100 cents where d = the value of a dime.

$\frac{100}{d} =$ _____ dimes

$d = \$0.$_____

$1

d

2. The distance of the Oregon Trail was about 2,000 mi long. This route would take settlers 4 months. Write a multiplication expression to show how many miles were crossed in a month on this route.

_____

_____

Three students are playing a math game. Each student gives a value for the variable in the expression and then evaluates the expression. The student with the greatest value wins the round. The students' variable values are given in the table.

Student	Value
Bobby	10
Hannah	2
Carlos	4

3. The first expression is $(3 + 7) \times (10 - \frac{n}{2})$. Who wins the round? What is the value of the expression?

_____

_____

4. The next expression is $\frac{(3n + 2)}{2}$. Who wins the round? What is the value of the expression?

_____

© Pearson Education, Inc. 4

Trying Triangles

Each of the smaller triangles stands for the
numbers 1–9. Use the expressions to identify
the values. Write the correct numbers in all of
the triangles. (Hint: Use try, check, and
revise as a strategy.)

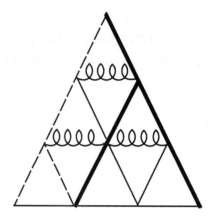

1.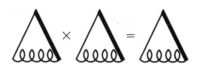

2.

3.

4.

5.

© Pearson Education, Inc. 4

Table That Rule

Below are some tables. Dewey, Corrie, and Isaac each try to
guess the rule. If the rule is correct, write *Yes.* If the rule is
incorrect, write the correct rule. Complete each table.

1. Dewey says, "The rule for this table is divide by 4."

Dewey's Table	16	32	56	48	12	18	24	30	n
	8	16	28						

_____

_____

2. Corrie says, "The rule for this table is multiply by 2, then
subtract 1."

Corrie's Table	7	2	6	4	12	3	10	5	11	n
	13	3	11							

_____

_____

3. Isaac says, "The rule for this table is add 1."

Isaac's Table	2	9	6	4	3	5	8	7	9	n
	3	24	15	9						

_____

_____

© Pearson Education, Inc. 4

Palm Tree Planning

The word *palm* refers to a group of flowering plants that have large, showy leaves. The ideal climate for palms is one that is warm and humid. However, all palms are not the same. Below is a chart of palms and some of their characteristics.

Palm	Maximum Height	Characteristics
Saw Palm	5 ft	ground creeper aggressive grower
Mediterranean Fan Palm	5 ft	small, clumping leaves slow grower
Palmetto Palm	90 ft	large trunk; leaves gather at top like cabbage
Windmill Palm	40 ft	fan-shaped leaves slender trunk

A landscaper is using the different characteristics of palm trees in order to plant the right palm in the best place. Use the chart of palm trees to help you plan the landscape.

1. Which palm would you plant in front of a house to provide shade?

   _____

2. Which palm would you plant to provide quick ground cover in a bare area?

   _____

3. Which palm would you plant to decorate and shade a spot on a patio?

   _____

4. Which palm would you plant to border both sides of a driveway?

   _____

© Pearson Education, Inc. 4

Minute by Minute

Examine the clocks in each group. Write the times shown in order
from earliest to latest. Assume that all the times shown are P.M.

1.

_____

2.

_____

3.

_____

4.

_____

© Pearson Education, Inc. 4

Time to Talk

Match the statement on the left to the correct response on the right.

We've gone 72 hours without electricity.

We usually get rid of them after $4\frac{1}{2}$ years.

I've owned the car for 54 months.

Yowsa—that's longer than most people live.

They said we might have to wait eight weeks for delivery.

Wow. Three days is a long time for that!

Her family has owned the land for over a century.

Really? That's over a quarter century.

I've had season tickets for three decades now.

One time I waited even longer than two months.

© Pearson Education, Inc. 4

It's About Time

Study each situation. Draw the hands on both clocks to show your estimate of how long each activity would take. Write A.M. or P.M. under each clock.

1.

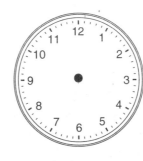

2.

3.

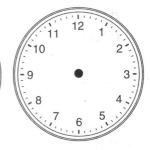

4.

© Pearson Education, Inc. 4

Who Wants Pizza?

Use the pizza menu to
answer the questions below.

Roger's Pizza

Order No.	Pizza Sizes	Number of People	Price
1	2 small pizzas	4	$8.95
2	1 large, 1 small	5	$11.95
3	1 large	3	$7.95
4	1 small	2	$5.95

1. Alexandra has $18.00.
   She wants enough pizza
   to feed 8 people. What
   should she order?

   _____

   _____

   _____

2. Carlos is buying lunch for himself. What should he get?

   _____

3. Julia is paying for order No. 2. Should she use a $10.00 bill
   or a $20.00 bill?

   _____

4. Andre pays for order No. 1 with a $20.00 bill. How much
   change will he get back?

   _____

5. On each table at the pizza restaurant
   is this sign. Bill ordered a small pizza
   with extra cheese. Cynthia, Derek, and
   Juanita ordered a large pizza. Who will
   eat first?

   _____

   _____

   _____

   How Long It Takes to Cook

Small Pizza	20 min
Large Pizza	30 min
Any pizza with extra cheese	Add 10 min

© Pearson Education, Inc. 4

Name_____

Let Me Check My Calendar

Larry is a very busy man. He often has to meet with salespeople in his department, as well as attend family functions. Study his appointment calendar below. Then tell whether each of Larry's statements is *True* or *False*.

July

S	M	T	W	T	F	S
1	2 Managers meeting 3–5	3	4	5 Presentation 1–3	6	7 Swimming party
8 Baseball game 2–5	9	10	11 Dentist 2:00	12	13 Workshop 8–4	14 Pick out furniture 1:00
15 BBQ NOON	16 Business trip to Denver Leave 6 A.M.	17	18 Home 8 P.M.	19	20 Sox game 7:15	21 Recital 12:00
22/29	23/30	24 Shop for gift after work	25	26	27 Day off— Mona's birthday	28

1. "I can meet with you about the new program on Tuesday the 10th, at around 2:00."   _____

2. "I'll be home the third Tuesday in July. Let's meet then."   _____

3. "No, I can't meet on the first Monday of the month. I have a big meeting."   _____

4. "Can I help you set up the new swing set on the 8th at around 3:00? Sure."   _____

5. "You can show me the new proposal after the meeting on the last Friday in July."   _____

6. "I'm free every Thursday morning this month."   _____

© Pearson Education, Inc. 4

Who Gets the Job?

Mr. Capello is opening up a new banquet hall. He needs to hire some busboys to clear tables. He also needs to hire a set-up crew to move and arrange tables and chairs for different banquets. Before hiring, Mr. Capello tested each of their skills. The results are shown in the pictographs below.

**Number of Tables
Set Up in 15 Minutes**

Dan	▢▢▢▢▢
Peter	▢▢
Will	▢▢▢
Sven	▢

Each ▢ = 4 tables

**Amount of Time
to Clear One Table**

Dan	○○◗
Peter	○○○○
Will	○○
Sven	◖

Each ○ = 1 minute

1. Which person should Mr. Capello immediately hire as a busboy? Why?

_____

_____

2. Which person would likely do a poor job as a busboy? Explain.

_____

_____

3. For which position would Mr. Capello most likely hire Dan? Why?

_____

_____

_____

© Pearson Education, Inc. 4

Plotting Solutions

Solve each equation.

1. $\frac{q}{2} = 7$

    $q =$ _____

2. $y + 2 = 18$

    $y =$ _____

3. $17 - r = 7$

    $r =$ _____

4. $8s = 88$

    $s =$ _____

5. $8 + 8 + w = 32$

    $w =$ _____

6. $p - 11 = 2$

    $p =$ _____

7. $4 \times a = 48$

    $a =$ _____

8. $\frac{144}{t} = 12$

    $t =$ _____

9. $k + 7 + 4 = 22$

    $k =$ _____

10. $\frac{200}{j} = 20$

    $j =$ _____

11. $73 - n = 59$

    $n =$ _____

12. $3h = 48$

    $h =$ _____

13. $\frac{750}{b} = 50$

    $b =$ _____

14. $x + 87 = 97$

    $x =$ _____

15. Complete the line plot of the solutions of Exercises 1–14. Are there any outliers?

_____

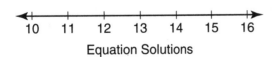

Equation Solutions

© Pearson Education, Inc. 4

Graphing True or False

Washington Elementary School kept a record of the number of books read by each grade in October. Gwen is using the data in the table to make a bar graph. Tell whether each statement is *True* or *False*.

Grade	2nd	3rd	4th	5th	6th
Books Read	395	419	461	443	511

1. Gwen's graph will have 5 bars. _____

2. The bar for 3rd grade will be twice as tall as the bar for 2nd grade. _____

3. The bar for each grade will have a greater length than the bar for the grade before. _____

4. The 6th grade bar will have the greatest length. _____

5. The title of Gwen's graph should be "Number of Books Read in November." _____

6. A good scale for Gwen's graph is 20. _____

7. Complete the bar graph using the data in the table.

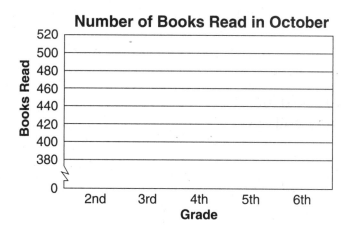

Number of Books Read in October

© Pearson Education, Inc. 4

Pictured Pairs

Draw a point for each ordered pair and label it.
Connect the points in letter order. Then connect
the last point to the first point.

1. A. (5, 9)

B. (7, 7)

C. (9, 5)

D. (7, 3)

E. (5, 1)

F. (5, 4)

G. (1, 4)

H. (1, 6)

I. (5, 6)

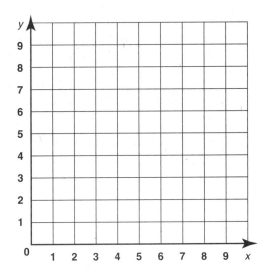

What is the picture? _____

2. A. (2, 2)

B. (1, 8)

C. (3, 5)

D. (4, 8)

E. (5, 5)

F. (6, 8)

G. (7, 5)

H. (9, 8)

I. (8, 2)

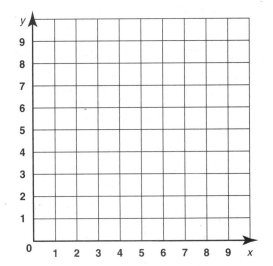

What is the picture? _____

© Pearson Education, Inc. 4

The Rice We Eat

The line graph shows the amount of rice eaten per person in the United States from 1983 to 1991. Use the graph to answer the questions. Circle the correct answer in Exercises 1–4.

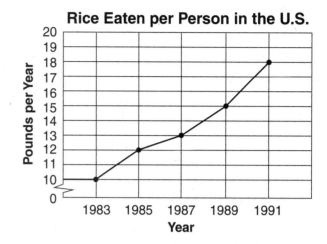

Rice Eaten per Person in the U.S.

1. Which of the following does the graph NOT show?

    A. That the amount of rice eaten per person was 2 lb more each year.

    B. That the amount of rice eaten per person increased over time.

    C. That more rice was eaten per person in 1989 than in 1983.

2. Between which two years did the amount of rice eaten per person increase the most?

    A. Between 1983 and 1985

    B. Between 1987 and 1989

    C. Between 1989 and 1991

3. Based on the graph, how much rice per person do you think was eaten in 1988?

    A. 15 lb

    B. 14 lb

    C. 13 lb

4. If the trend shown in the graph continued, how much rice was eaten per person in 1993 compared to 1991?

    A. More

    B. Less

    C. The same

© Pearson Education, Inc. 4

Mystery Machines

Figure out the mystery in each machine below. A number goes in and another number goes out. Find what happens to the number in the machine. Write down each pattern. Then fill in the blank boxes.

1.

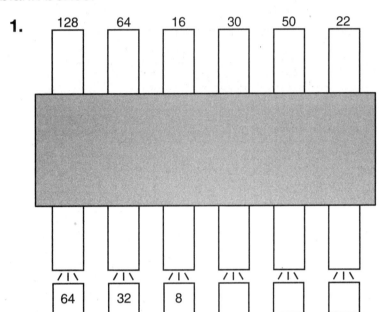

128	64	16	30	50	22
64	32	8			

2.

1	4	3	8	6	10
48	51	50			

© Pearson Education, Inc. 4

Name_____

Special Numbers

Use the clues below to find the special number in each shape.
Each clue tells you a number that is NOT the special number.

1.

8	36	95	
11	48	29	60

It is not the mean of 32, 35, 38, and 39.
It is not the quotient of 48 and 6.
It is not the product of 5 and 12.
It is not the median of 22, 25, 28, 29, 31, 45, and 67.
It is not the sum of 43 and 52.
It is not the mode of 11, 23, 3, 11, 43, 3, 27, 11, and 91.

The special number is _____.

2.

7	26		
	19		44
	140	11	62

It is not the mode of 2, 19, 6, 17, 19, 43, 29, 19, and 17.
It is not the difference of 81 and 19.
It is not the quotient of 77 and 11.
It is not the mean of 18, 25, 34, 22, 91, 54, and 64.
It is not the product of 7 and 20.
It is not the median of 3, 4, 5, 6, 11, 12, 13, 14, and 18.

The special number is _____.

© Pearson Education, Inc. 4

Scattered Puzzle

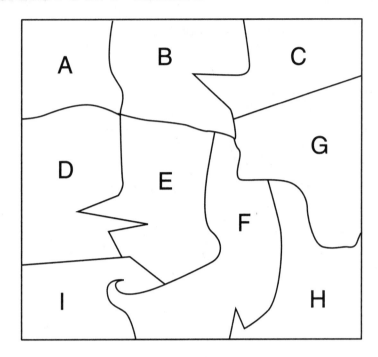

Write the letter of each puzzle piece from the completed puzzle above in each piece below.

© Pearson Education, Inc. 4

Do Pictures Tell the Whole Story?

Use the data in the table below to make a misleading graph.

**Books Missing from
the School Library**

Year	Books Missing
1998	7
1999	6
2000	8
2001	12
2002	11
2003	6

1. Make a graph that makes the change in missing library
   books appear very great.

2. Why would someone want to create a graph that is
   misleading? Explain your answer.

   _____

   _____

   _____

© Pearson Education, Inc. 4

Saving Red Wolves

In North America, there are two kinds of wolves. Gray wolves live almost everywhere, but red wolves live only in the southeastern United States. By 1970, only about 100 red wolves lived along the coast of Texas and Louisiana. Many of the wolves were a mix of red wolves and coyotes, so people thought the red wolf was extinct. The Alligator River National Wildlife Refuge in North Carolina began trying to save the red wolf. Scientists captured some wolves to help them, but only a small number of the captured wolves were true red wolves. In 1988, the first pair of true red wolves was released into the refuge. Today, about 100 red wolves live there.

Solve each problem. Write your answer in a complete sentence.

1. How many more red wolves are there in the refuge today than in 1988?

_____

_____

2. Red wolves are smaller than gray wolves. While a red wolf might weigh as much as 80 lb, a gray wolf can be 95 lb heavier. How much can a gray wolf weigh?

_____

3. If the refuge captured 400 animals and only 14 were true red wolves, how many of the animals were not true red wolves?

_____

4. Wolves usually have litters of 1 to 11 pups. If 8 wolves had pups in one month, what is the greatest number of pups there could be?

_____

© Pearson Education, Inc. 4

In the Blink of an Eye

1. You take about 4,000 steps in 12 hr. About how many steps do you take in 8 days? Fill in the table. Look for a pattern.

Time	12 hr	24 hr	2 days	4 days	8 days
Number of Steps					

2. About how many steps do you take in a 30-day month? Explain how you found your answer.

_____

_____

3. You breathe about 10 times every 30 sec. About how many times do you breathe in 10 hr? Fill in the table. Look for a pattern.

Time	30 sec	1 min	10 min	1 hr	10 hr
Number of Breaths					

4. About how many times do you breathe in a day? Explain how you found your answer.

_____

_____

5. Your eyes blink about 150 times in 10 min. About how many times do you blink in 3 min? Fill in the table. Look for a pattern.

Time	10 min	5 min	4 min	3 min	2 min	1 min
Number of Blinks						

6. About how many times do your eyes blink every 30 sec? Explain how the table you made can help you find the answer.

_____

_____

© Pearson Education, Inc. 4

Who's Here?

Do you know how to find the attendance of people at a large
event? It is too many people to count one-by-one, so you need
to use an estimate. This is called crowd estimation.

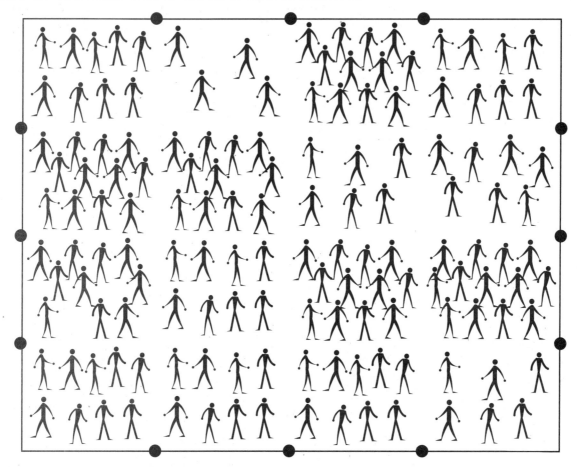

1. Draw 3 lines going up and down. Connect dot to
   dot. Draw 3 lines going across. Connect dot to dot.
   Find the box that is farthest left and on the bottom.
   Count as many people in the box as you can.   _____

2. Count the total number of boxes.   _____

3. Estimate to find the total number of people.

   number of people × number of boxes = total number of people

   _____ × _____ = _____

© Pearson Education, Inc. 4

Block Party

Find the pattern of blocks in each structure. Then write the total number of blocks.

1. There are 3 levels.

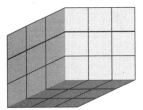

Total number of blocks: _____

2. There are 5 levels.

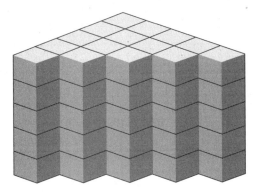

Total number of blocks: _____

3. Copy the pattern of 3 shaded blocks, 2 spotted blocks, and 1 striped block. Repeat this pattern to draw a side view of a staircase with 12 shaded blocks, 8 striped blocks, and 4 spotted blocks.

Pattern: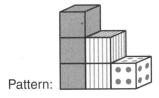

© Pearson Education, Inc. 4

Thanks a Bunch

It is time for you to bring the vegetables from your garden to a farmer's market. Your stand can only hold 500 lb. The vegetables have already been packaged in bunches or groups. Decide what you want to bring and how much money you want to earn. Fill in the Farmer's Market Tally Sheet to keep track of all your choices, weights, and money.

Farmer's Market Vegetables

Vegetable	Weight per Package	Packages Available	Price per Package
Broccoli	3 lb	20	$5
Carrots	2 lb	32	$6
Cucumbers	6 lb	19	$7
Lettuce	1 lb	72	$2
Peppers	5 lb	53	$7
Tomatoes	4 lb	41	$5

Farmer's Market Tally Sheet

Vegetable	Number of Packages	Weight of Packages	$ Amount of Packages

Total weight: _____   Total $ amount: _____

1. What was the total weight of all the produce you brought to the market?

_____

_____

© Pearson Education, Inc. 4

Name_____

Mathematical Marlena

Marlena is about to amaze you with great feats of mathematics.
Marlena says, "I want you to write the number 37 three times."

1. Now she says, "Multiply the first 37 by 1." _____

2. Then she tells you, "Multiply the second 37 by 2." _____

3. She directs you to, "Multiply the third 37 by 3." _____

4. She says, "Take each product and multiply it by 3."

_____

_____

5. Marlena now asks, "What is the pattern through the number 9?"

_____

_____

Then Marlena begins her second math game.

6. She tells you, "Write a number between 1 and 5." _____

7. Then she says, "Now add 5 to the number." _____

8. Now she says, "Multiply the number by 2." _____

9. She says, "Subtract 2 from the product." _____

10. Marlena then says, "Now multiply that answer by 2." _____

11. Then she asks you to, "Divide the product by 4." _____

12. She finally directs you to, "Subtract 4 from your answer." _____

Marlena says, "The answer is the number you wrote down!"

© Pearson Education, Inc. 4

Name_____

Roll Out the Fun

Find the missing factors and products to complete the number sentences. Then complete the sentences in the word problems.

Zippy Roller Coaster	Souvenirs
Height: 83 ft Length: 903 ft	Baseball cap—157 tickets T-shirt—279 tickets Stuffed animal—318 tickets

1. $109 \times 2 =$ _____ $139 \times 2 =$ _____

Neil's family and Reena's family spent two days at the amusement park. On Fridays, family passes cost $109. On Saturdays, family passes cost $139. Altogether, the two

families spent _____ on Friday and _____ on Saturday.

2. _____ $\times 9 =$ _____ $83 \times$ _____ $=$ _____

The world's longest roller coaster is 9 times the length of the Zippy roller coaster. The world's highest roller coaster is about 5 times the height of the Zippy roller coaster. The

world's longest roller coaster is _____ ft long. The

world's highest roller coaster is _____ ft high.

3. $157 \times$ _____ $=$ _____   _____ $\times 2 =$ _____

Before leaving the amusement park, Reena went to the souvenir store. She got 1 baseball cap for each of her 3 friends. Then she bought herself 2 stuffed animals. Reena

used _____ tickets to get gifts for her friends and

_____ tickets to get the stuffed animals.

© Pearson Education, Inc. 4

Make a Guess

First, guess the number of digits that will be in each product.
Then, solve the problem and write the actual number of digits.
Finally, explain why your guess might have been different from
the actual number.

1. 54
$\times$ 7

Guess: There are _____ digits.

Actual: There are _____ digits.

Explanation: _____

_____

_____

2. 236
$\times$ 5

Guess: There are _____ digits.

Actual: There are _____ digits.

Explanation: _____

_____

_____

3. 5,000
$\times$ 9

Guess: There are _____ digits.

Actual: There are _____ digits.

Explanation: _____

_____

_____

© Pearson Education, Inc. 4

Name_____

Clue Me In

"It is what you have in common with about 10 million other people."

To solve the riddle, you must follow all of the clues. Use the map to discover where each clue takes you.

					A		Y
D							
			T				
					I		
		R					
			H				
★							
		B					

N
↑
W ←●→ E
↓
S

1. **Clue 1:** From the star, go 3 blocks east and 1 block south. _____

2. **Clue 2:** Go 4 blocks east, 4 blocks north, and 1 block west. _____

3. **Clue 3:** Go west 4 blocks and then south 1 block. _____

4. **Clue 4:** Go north 2 blocks and then 1 block east. _____

5. **Clue 5:** Go 1 block east and then three blocks south. _____

6. **Clue 6:** Go 4 blocks west and then go 4 blocks north. _____

7. **Clue 7:** Go 5 blocks east and 1 block north. _____

8. **Clue 8:** Go 2 blocks east. _____

9. Place the letters in the order of the clues to solve the riddle.

_____

© Pearson Education, Inc. 4

Name_____

It All Makes Cents

A nine-year-old earns an average of $7.00 each week in allowance.

Country	1 month Saves	1 month Spends	6 months Saves	6 months Spends	12 months Saves	12 months Spends
China	$18.20	$12.13				
France	$9.10	$21.23				
Germany	$13.95	$16.38				
Japan	$18.80	$11.53				
United Kingdom	$7.89	$22.45				
United States	$6.37	$23.96				

1. Find out how much allowance a 9-year-old from each country saves and spends in 6 months and 12 months. Write your answers in the chart.

2. Round each savings and spending to the nearest tens place for 12 months.

12 Months

Country	Saves	Spends
China		
France		
Germany		
Japan		
United Kingdom		
United States		

Use your estimated totals to answer the questions.

3. In which country do children spend 3 times more allowance than they save?

_____

4. In which country does a child save 2 times more allowance than a child from France?

_____

© Pearson Education, Inc. 4

Building Factors

Multiply to solve each problem.

Luisa lives in an apartment building. The building has 3 floors. On each floor lives a family of 5. The 1st floor has a family with 2 parents and 3 children. The 2nd floor has 2 grandparents and 3 children. The 3rd floor has 1 parent and 1 grandmother and 3 children.

Each person in the building has 2 pairs of shoes.

1. How many pairs of shoes are in the building?

_____

_____

The adults on all 3 floors each have 3 books from the library.

2. How many books from the library are in the building?

_____

_____

The children on the 1st floor and the children on the 3rd floor each have 6 compact discs.

3. How many compact discs are in the building?

_____

_____

The adults on the 1st floor and the adults on the 2nd floor and 2 children on the 3rd floor each have 7 pairs of white socks.

4. How many pairs of white socks are in the building?

_____

_____

© Pearson Education, Inc. 4

Name_____

How Many Are There?

Use addition, subtraction, or multiplication to find the number of each shape in the patterns in the figures below. Then explain how you found your answers.

1.

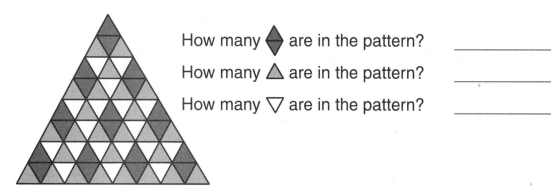

How many ◆ are in the pattern? _____

How many △ are in the pattern? _____

How many ▽ are in the pattern? _____

How did you find the number of each shape in the pattern?

_____

_____

_____

2.

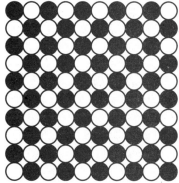

How many ✧ are in the pattern? _____

How many ● are in the pattern? _____

How many ○ are in the pattern? _____

How did you find the number of each shape in the pattern?

_____

_____

_____

© Pearson Education, Inc. 4

Math in Ancient History

The ancient Egyptians had a writing system based on hieroglyphs. Hieroglyphs are pictures that represent words or numbers. The Egyptians had separate place-value symbols for 1 unit, 1 ten, 1 hundred, and so on. Here is the number 276 written in hieroglyphs.

1. Decide which Egyptian place value symbols stand for 276. Use what you know to solve the multiplication sentence below, using hieroglyphs.

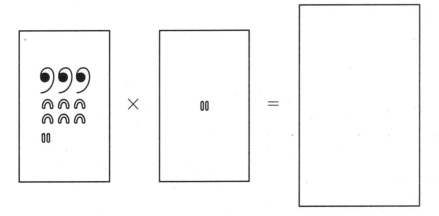

2. The ancient Egyptians used the symbol X to stand for 1 thousand. Use what you have learned about ancient Egyptian symbols to solve the multiplication sentence below using hieroglyphs.

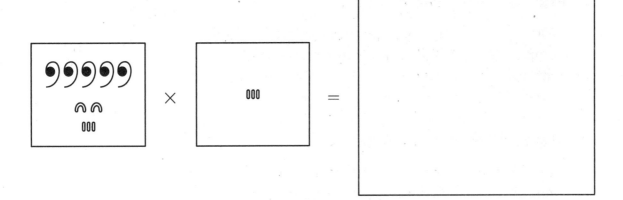

© Pearson Education, Inc. 4

Name_____

The World's Greatest

World's sleepiest animal

1 min	=	60 sec
1 hr	=	60 min
1 month	=	28–31 days
1 year	=	12 months
1 decade	=	10 years
1 century	=	100 years

1. A koala sleeps about 20 hr each day. How many hours does it sleep in the month of June?

_____

World's Number 1 milk drinking country

2. Each person in Ireland drinks about 700 c of milk each year. How many cups would each person drink in 5 decades?

_____

World's fastest orbiting planet

3. Mercury orbits the sun in 88 days. The planet travels about 30 mi in 1 sec. How far does the planet travel in 1 min?

_____

World's busiest airport

4. Hartsfield Atlanta International Airport in Georgia has about 2,000 airplanes depart and arrive each day. How many times do planes land and take off in April?

_____

World's coldest populated place

5. Norilsk is a small city in central Russia. The average temperature is 12.4°F. The city has 5 months without sunlight each year. How many months without sunlight occur in 1 century?

_____

World's heaviest land mammal

6. The African elephant weighs about 14,000 lb. It eats about 50,000 lb of twigs, foliage, grasses, and fruit in 3 months. How many pounds of food does it eat in 1 year?

_____

© Pearson Education, Inc. 4

Vacation Estimation

Mileage Between Cities

	Miami	New York City	Pittsburgh	Washington, D.C.
Miami	—	1,328	1,250	1,101
New York City	1,328	—	386	229
Pittsburgh	1,250	386	—	241
Washington, D.C.	1,101	229	241	—

It is 9:00 A.M. Your family vacation starts in New York City with a final destination in Miami, Florida. You travel 58 mi every hour if you do not stop for meals or attractions. You first head to Washington, D.C.

1. You must stop for a 1 hr lunch at noon. Use rounding to estimate how many miles you have traveled by noon.

_____

2. Estimate how far away you are from Washington, D.C.

_____

3. You arrive in Washington, D.C. You do some sightseeing, and at 5:00 P.M. you continue your trip and drive until 7:00 P.M. You stop for dinner and rest for the evening. Estimate how many miles you have driven for the day.

_____

4. Your family starts the second day at 9:00 A.M. and drives until 8:00 P.M. During that time, you stopped for 2 hr. Estimate how far you traveled for the day.

_____

5. Estimate how far you are from Miami.

_____

6. On the third day, about what time must you leave in the morning to get to Miami around 5:00 P.M.? Remember, you will stop for a 1 hr lunch.

_____

© Pearson Education, Inc. 4

Crazy Cubes

Write the letter of the cube that is not the same as the others in the group.

1. A   B   C

_____

2. A   C

B   D

_____

3. A   B   C

D   E   F

_____

4. A   B   C

D   E   F

_____

© Pearson Education, Inc. 4

Separate the Dots

Draw line segments inside each circle so that each dot is in a separate area. The 2 ends of each line segment must touch the circle.

1. Draw 2 line segments to separate the dots.

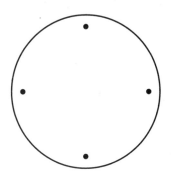 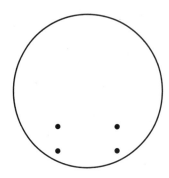

2. Draw 3 line segments to separate the dots.

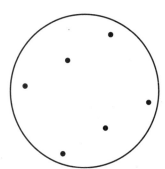 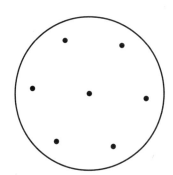

3. Draw 4 line segments to separate the dots.

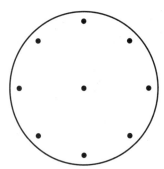 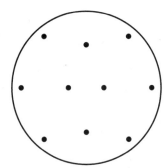

© Pearson Education, Inc. 4

Food for Thought

You work at a pet shop. One of your jobs is to feed all the animals. Answer the questions below.

First thing in the morning you feed the fish. The 12 fish tanks have 26 large fish. You can choose between two kinds of pellets.

Daily Feeding Chart

Fish	10 super pellets each or 21 mini pellets each
Puppies	16 oz dry food each or 14 oz wet food each

1. Which kind of pellets do you choose? Estimate the number of pellets you need. Explain your method.

   _____

   _____

   _____

2. What is the exact amount?

   _____

   _____

You feed the puppies next. There are 10 cages of large-breed puppies. Each cage can hold 3 puppies, but 2 of the cages only have 2 puppies each. You need to decide which food to give the puppies.

3. What kind of puppy food do you choose? Estimate the amount of puppy food you need. Explain your method.

   _____

   _____

4. What is the exact amount?

   _____

   _____

© Pearson Education, Inc. 4

Treasure!

Benjamin is a treasure hunter. He and his crew recently found the treasure of a sunken ship from the past. The chests contained gold, silver, and jewels.

Treasure Found

Type of Chest	Weight of Each Chest	Number of Each Chest
Gold	178 lb	58
Silver	153 lb	53
Jewels	123 lb	29

Benjamin's ship can carry a maximum weight of 10,000 lb without sinking.

1. What is the total weight of the gold chests? _____

2. What is the total weight of the silver chests? _____

3. What is the total weight of the jewel chests? _____

4. How many trips does Benjamin need to take to carry all of the chests to shore? How do you know?

_____

_____

_____

5. Suppose Benjamin only carries gold chests on his last trip. If Benjamin carried full loads on the first two trips, about how many gold chests will he carry on the last trip?

_____

_____

_____

© Pearson Education, Inc. 4

Name_____

The Skateboard Business

Dave is interested in the skateboard business. He found
out the following information about some companies that
produce skateboards.

Skateboard Manufacturers

Manufacturers	Daily Production	Days of Operation
Big Z Skateboards	4,240	Tuesday through Saturday
California Super Boards	3,892	Closed on Sundays
Rocket Rides	3,725	Open every day of the year
Wonder Wheels	5,000	Monday through Thursday

Solve the problems below using mental math, paper and pencil,
or calculator. Tell which method you used.

1. Which company manufactures the most skateboards in
   2 days? How many skateboards does that company make?

   _____

2. Starting on Monday, which company will make more
   skateboards in 5 days, Big Z or California Super Boards?
   Write the total number each company will make.

   _____

   _____

   _____

3. Starting on Friday, which company will make the most
   skateboards in 10 days? Write the total number all of the
   companies will make.

   _____

   _____

   _____

© Pearson Education, Inc. 4

Name_____

Bogus Bucks

Rosa deciphers codes. A bank has hired her to crack the codes on 7 safes. The codes also tell the amount of money in each safe.

Decipher the codes using the following information:

A = 1, B = 2, C = 3, and so on.

Use the clues below to find out how much money is in each safe. Write each amount on the correct safe.

Clue 1: $0.80 × BC is on top

Clue 2: $2.10 × FA is below left of $0.80 × BC

Clue 3: $3.45 × AG is right and 2 above $6.09 × H

Clue 4: $4.61 × BI is above and left of $1.78 × DE

Clue 5: $5.55 × CC is right and above $6.09 × H

Clue 6: $6.09 × H is 2 safes below $2.10 × FA

Clue 7: $1.78 × DE is below and right of $4.61 × BI

1.

_____

2.   3.

_____   _____

4. 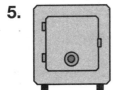   5.

_____   _____

6. 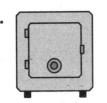   7.

_____   _____

© Pearson Education, Inc. 4

Fun For Eight, Eight For Fun

The Amazing Zellmar calls you up to the stage.

- He wants you to think of a number between 1 and 20.

- He tells you to multiply the number by 2.

- Now add 8 to the number.

- Amazing Zellmar says to divide or split the result in half.

- He tells you to subtract the original number from your answer.

- Now he says to take that number and multiply it by 111.

- Finally, he tells you to take your answer and multiply it by 11.

1. Zellmar says to look at the title of this page. How does it relate to the answer to the problem you just did?

_____

_____

_____

2. Why do you think everyone got the same answer?

_____

_____

_____

_____

_____

© Pearson Education, Inc. 4

Next?

Draw the next two shapes to continue the pattern.

1.

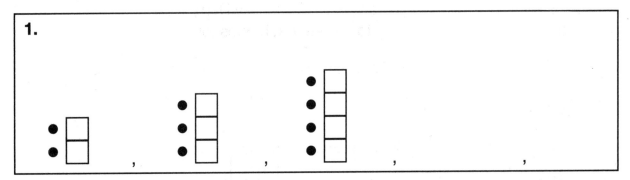

2.

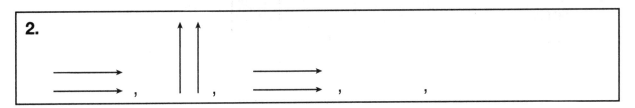

3.

4. WW. , WW. , WW'W. ,

5.

6.

© Pearson Education, Inc. 4

Name_____

Barry's Best Sellers

The graph below shows the titles of the four best-selling books at Barry's Book Store. It also shows how much money Barry made from each book. Divide mentally to answer each question.

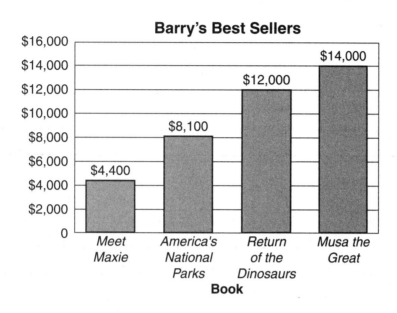

Barry's Best Sellers

1. Barry charged $7 for each copy of *Musa the Great*. How many total copies did Barry sell? _____

2. Barry charged $4 for each copy of *Return of the Dinosaurs*. How many total copies did Barry sell? _____

3. Barry charged $9 for each copy of *America's National Parks*. How many total copies did Barry sell? _____

4. Barry began charging $5 for each copy of *Meet Maxie*. He then lowered the price to $4 a copy. How many total copies might Barry have sold? Circle the most reasonable amount listed below.

   700   800   900

5. Which book did Barry sell the most copies of?

   _____

© Pearson Education, Inc. 4

Franny's To-Do List

Franny wants to get a lot done this weekend. She made a list of things she needs to do.

Franny's To-Do List
- Put pictures in photo album.
- Finish reading book.
- Buy presents for Kate, Wong, and Tia.
- Put CDs on rack.

1. Franny wants to place the remaining 64 photos in a large photo album. She has 5 pages left in the album. About how many photos can she place on each page?

   _____

2. Franny has to read 113 pages to finish her book. She plans to spend 4 hr reading. About how many pages should she read each hour to finish the book?

   _____

3. Franny wants to spend an equal amount of money on the presents for her 3 friends. If she has $53, about how much money can she spend on each present?

   _____

4. Franny's new CD rack has 8 rows. If Franny has 130 CDs, about how many can she put on each row?

   _____

© Pearson Education, Inc. 4

Order Lunch

Liz invited some friends to her house for lunch. She is ordering food from Daisy's Diner down the street. She is thinking of buying one of the party-sized items listed in the chart.

Food Item	Amount	Serving Size
Texas Chili	38 oz	8 oz
Deluxe Veggie Pizza	16 slices	3 slices
Corn-Cob Delight	18 cobs	4 cobs

1. How many people can Liz serve if she buys the Texas Chili? _____

   How many ounces will she have left over? _____

2. How many people can Liz serve if she buys the Deluxe Veggie Pizza? _____

   How many slices will she have left over? _____

3. How many people can Liz serve if she buys the Corn-Cob Delight? _____

   How many corn cobs will she have left over? _____

4. Liz needs to buy enough food for 5 people. She does not want to have a lot of food left over. What should she buy? _____

5. The Texas Chili costs $11.99; the Deluxe Pizza costs $15.50; the Corn-Cob Delight cost $17.75. Do these prices change your decision about what Liz should buy? Explain your answer.

   _____

© Pearson Education, Inc. 4

Will They Reach the Top?

Begin at the bottom of each mountain and solve each multiplication problem. If there is a remainder, the hiker stops at that problem. If there is no remainder, the hiker keeps climbing.

1.

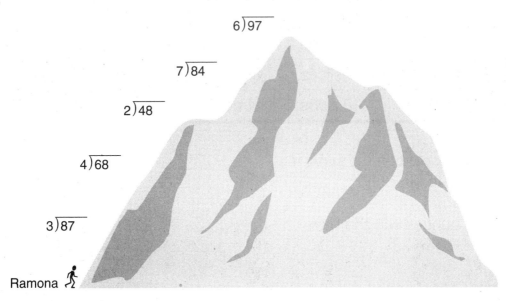

$6\overline{)97}$

$7\overline{)84}$

$2\overline{)48}$

$4\overline{)68}$

$3\overline{)87}$

Ramona

2.

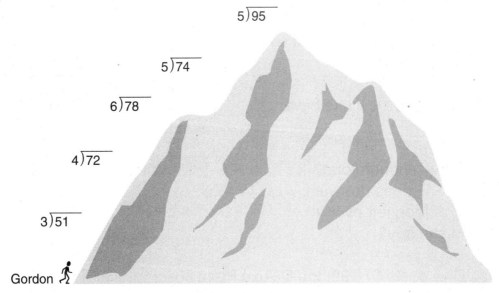

$5\overline{)95}$

$5\overline{)74}$

$6\overline{)78}$

$4\overline{)72}$

$3\overline{)51}$

Gordon

3. Which hiker made it farther up the mountain?

_____

© Pearson Education, Inc. 4

Name_____

New Shapes

If you place the figure on the left inside of the figure on the right, what would the new figure look like? Circle the letter of the figure that shows the new figure.

1.

   A. **B.** **C.**

2.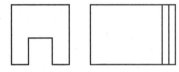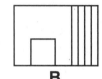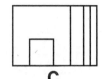

   A. **B.** **C.**

3.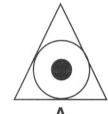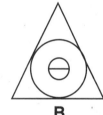

   A. **B.** **C.**

4.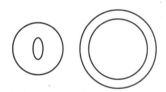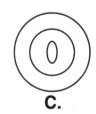

   A. **B.** **C.**

5.

   A. **B.** **C.**

© Pearson Education, Inc. 4

Name_____

Rapunzel's Hair

Rapunzel's hair is 83 in. long! She wants to use her hair to make some wigs to sell.

1.

Suppose the hair on each wig is 6 in. long. How many wigs can Rapunzel make?

_____

How long will her hair be after she cuts it?

_____

2.

Rapunzel grows her hair out to 59 in. long. She cuts her hair to make more wigs. The hair on each wig needs to be 3 in. long. How many wigs can she make?

_____

How long will her hair be after she cuts it?

_____

3.

Rapunzel decides to not make wigs for a long time. Her hair grows to 94 in. long! Then she decides to make more wigs. The length of the hair on each wig needs to be 8 in. long. How many wigs can she make?

_____

© Pearson Education, Inc. 4

Name_____

The History of Zoro

Use the time line to answer the questions below.

Important Dates in Zoro's History

1503: Zoro is founded

1507: First presidential election

1603: Centennial celebration

1819: First Zoro Olympics

1. A new president is elected every 4 years. By the year 2004, how many presidents will Zoro have had?

_____

2. The people of Zoro decided they would continue to hold their Olympics every 6 years. By the year 2004, how many Olympics will Zoro have had?

_____

3. Based on the time line, what do you think a Centennial celebration is for?

_____

_____

4. What other event would have occurred in the year of the Centennial celebration?

_____

5. Tina Jones was the first figure skater to obtain a perfect score in the Zoro Olympics. This happened during the 6th Zoro Olympics. In what year did this take place?

_____

© Pearson Education, Inc. 4

Name_____

Stop the Flood!

The river is overflowing! If a dam is not built, the towns downstream will be flooded.

Solve each division problem below. If the quotient does not have a zero, draw a dam from the quotient across the river.

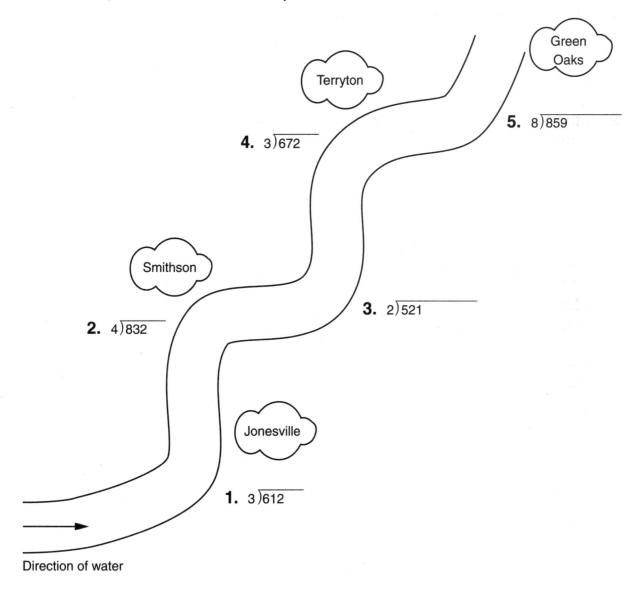

6. Which town or towns will NOT be flooded?

_____

© Pearson Education, Inc. 4

Name_____

Making Money

"Money! Let's earn some money!" That was what 6 friends decided to do one summer afternoon. They set up a window-washing business. After 3 days of washing windows, they earned a total of $7.50.

1. The group divided the money equally among all 6 people. How much did each person receive?

    _____

2. If there were only 5 friends, how much did each person receive?

    _____

    "I think we can make more if we divide into 2 different companies," Mary said. So they did. Mary and Stan formed Company A. They washed windows and earned a total of $8.54. The other 4 friends formed Company B. They sold lemonade and earned a total of $8.92.

3. The 2 companies each divided their earnings equally among all company members. How much did each person earn in each company?

    _____

4. Do you think Mary made a wise decision? Why or why not?

    _____

    _____

    _____

5. If there were 3 friends in each company, how much did each person earn?

    _____

© Pearson Education, Inc. 4

The Mixed Up Patterns

Draw or write what comes next in the patterns below.

1. 10, △, 12, △ △, ____, _____

2. ★ ★★, 24, ★ ★, 12, _____, ____

3. A ▯ B, C ▯▯ D, E ▯▯▯ F, _____ _____

4. 200, ○○○○, 150, ○○○, 100, _____, _____

5. 555, 44P, 666, 33Q, _____, _____

6. XXOX, XOOX, XXOX, _____, _____

7. ▢, 99, ▢▢, 88, ▢▢▢, _____, _____

8. 13, ↑10, 23, ↑100, 123, _____, _____

© Pearson Education, Inc. 4

Name_____

Safe Passage by Numbers

Felicia is backpacking and must cross three rivers to reach the campsite. Write *yes* or *no* in each blank to state if the number is divisible by the two numbers at the start of each trail. She cannot cross the river if there are any *no* answers on the trail.

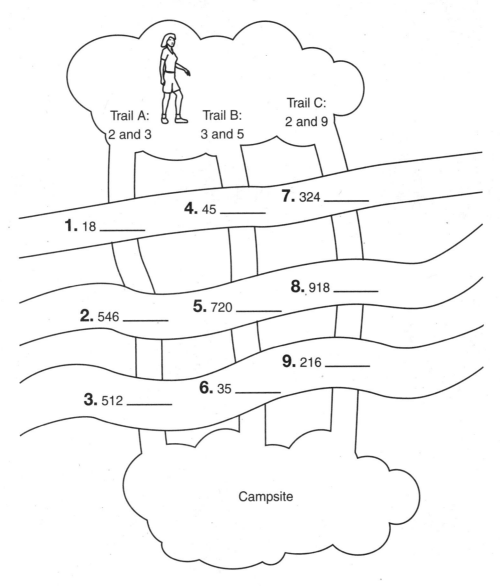

Trail A: 2 and 3

Trail B: 3 and 5

Trail C: 2 and 9

7. 324 _____

4. 45 _____

1. 18 _____

8. 918 _____

5. 720 _____

2. 546 _____

9. 216 _____

6. 35 _____

3. 512 _____

Campsite

10. Which trail must Felicia take to reach the campsite? _____

11. Find a divisibility rule for 4 and 6.

_____

_____

_____

© Pearson Education, Inc. 4

Name_____

The Jumping Frogs

Frankfort has a frog-jumping contest each year. Diego hopes to have the winning frog. He caught three frogs from the swamp and had them each take three leaps.

1. First, make an estimate. Based on the distances shown, which frog should Diego enter in the contest? Why do you think so?

   _____

   _____

2. Frog A

   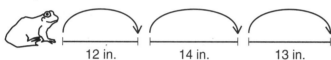

   12 in.   14 in.   13 in.

   What is the average leap of Frog A?   _____

3. Frog B

   6 in.   20 in.   10 in.

   What is the average leap of Frog B?   _____

4. Frog C

   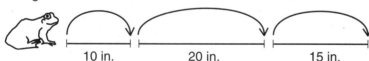

   10 in.   20 in.   15 in.

   What is the average leap of Frog C?   _____

5. Based on the actual average leap, which frog should Diego enter in the contest? Why do you think so?

   _____

   _____

© Pearson Education, Inc. 4

Add or Subtract?

Solve each division problem using mental math. If the answer has one zero, write an addition sign in the box. If the answer has two zeros, write a subtraction sign in the box. Then compute the numbers in the column on the right.

1. $8,100 \div 9$ = _____ ☐ 500
   100

2. $5,600 \div 7$ = _____ ☐ 200

3. $3,200 \div 80$ = _____ ☐ 60

4. $1,500 \div 30$ = _____ ☐ 40

5. $2,400 \div 4$ = _____ ☐ 100

6. $5,400 \div 60$ = _____ ☐ 200

7. $1,800 \div 30$ = _____ ☐ 300

8. $4,900 \div 7$ = _____ ☐ 500

9. $3,600 \div 90$ = _____ ☐ 400

10. $1,500 \div 3$ = _____ ☐ 70

11. $4,800 \div 6$ = _____ ☐ 30

12. $2,700 \div 9$ = _____ ☐ 100

13. What number did you get after computing the numbers in the right-hand column?

   _____

© Pearson Education, Inc. 4

What's His Mood?

Complete each division problem. Then follow the directions
after the problem.

1. 15)183

2. If the quotient has a
remainder, draw a line
from M to O. If not, draw a
line from N to L.

3. 22)352

4. If the quotient has a
remainder, draw a line
from B to F. If not, draw a
line from B to E.

5. 47)799

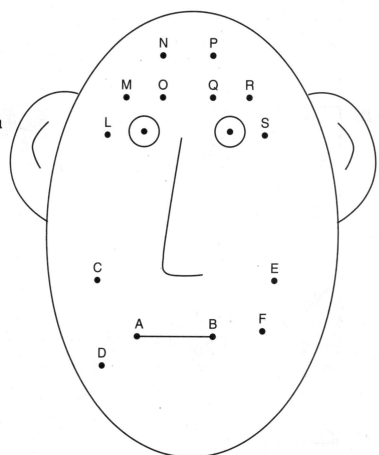

6. If the quotient has a remainder, draw a line from P to S.
If not, draw a line from Q to R.

7. 33)384

8. If the quotient has a remainder, draw a line from
A to C. If not, draw a line from A to D.

9. Is the man happy or sad? _____

© Pearson Education, Inc. 4

Name_____

I Can See It in the Flag!

Which flag does each shape appear in? Write the letter of the
flag next to each shape.

A.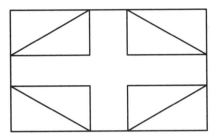

D.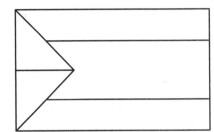

B.

E.

C.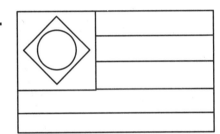

F.

1.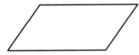

_____

2.

_____

3.

_____

4.

_____

5.

_____

6.

_____

© Pearson Education, Inc. 4

Use with Lesson 7-15. **95**

Name_____

It's Just Solid Fun

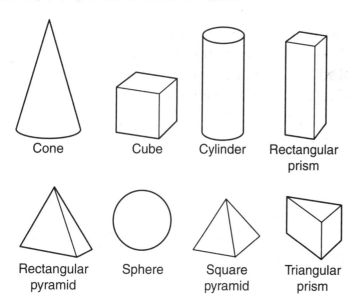

Cone   Cube   Cylinder   Rectangular
                                  prism

Rectangular   Sphere   Square   Triangular
pyramid   pyramid   prism

Write an equation for each exercise. Use *f* for the number of
faces, *e* for the number of edges, and *v* for the number of vertices.

1. In a cube, how does the number of faces
   compare to the number of edges?   _____

2. What is the relationship of the number of edges
   and the number of vertices in a cube?   _____

3. Compare the number of faces in a cube to the
   number of vertices in a cube.   _____

4. In a triangular prism, what is the relationship
   between the number of faces and the number
   of edges?   _____

5. What equation could you write to compare the
   number of faces to the number of vertices in a
   rectangular pyramid?   _____

6. In a triangular prism, how does the number of
   faces compare to the number of vertices? _____

7. What is the relationship between the number
   of faces in a rectangular pyramid and the
   number of edges?   _____

© Pearson Education, Inc. 4

Name_____

Playground Numbers

The Wellington School needs to raise money for a new playground climber. The 4th grade needs to raise at least $150 for their share. They have estimated how much they can earn from a number of activities. For Exercises 1–4, tell which of the listed activities you would vote to do. Explain why you chose those activities. Then write the total amount of money that would be earned if the estimates are accurate.

1. Bake sale: $85
   Car wash: $93
   Put on a play: $75
   Sell juice at the basketball game: $59

   _____

   _____

2. Craft sale: $98
   Book sale: $65
   Student artwork sale: $70
   Make and sell a school directory: $80

   _____

   _____

3. Pancake breakfast: $80
   Make and sell a school calendar: $73
   Sell lemonade at Sports Day: $65
   Walk-a-thon: $59

   _____

   _____

4. What other things besides money are important to consider when deciding on activities? List at least two.

   _____

   _____

© Pearson Education, Inc. 4

Street Smarts

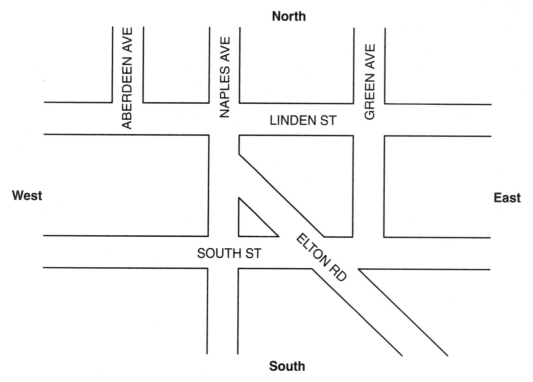

1. Name 2 streets that run north and south, intersect South Street, and are parallel to each other.

   _____

2. Name 2 streets that are parallel and run east and west.

   _____

3. Name a street that intersects Linden Street at a right angle and intersects no other street.

   _____

4. Name a street that intersects South Street, but NOT at a right angle.

   _____

5. Three parallel streets intersect an east-west street at right angles. Name the east-west street.

   _____

© Pearson Education, Inc. 4

Name_____

Doodles

Darius made this doodle while talking on the phone. Name each shape Darius drew. Be as specific as possible.

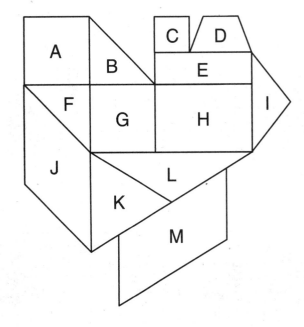

A. _____

B. _____

C. _____

D. _____

E. _____

F. _____

G. _____

H. _____

I. _____

J. _____

K. _____

L. _____

M. _____

© Pearson Education, Inc. 4

Name_____

Don't Look Now!

Geometric figures are hidden in the boxes below. You can't look!
The information in each exercise will allow you to figure out what
each box contains. For each exercise, write which figure is in each
box. You may write in the boxes to help you solve each exercise.

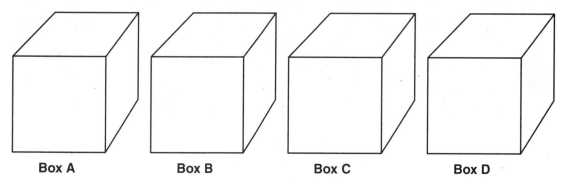

Box A   **Box B**   **Box C**   **Box D**

1. Hidden figures: right triangle, rectangle, isosceles triangle, parallelogram
   The quadrilaterals are next to each other.
   The figures in Boxes A and C have right angles.

   The isosceles triangle is in Box B.

   Box A: _____   Box B: _____

   Box C: _____   Box D: _____

2. Hidden figures: sphere, cone, cylinder, cube
   Box A contains a solid that rolls.
   The cube is in Box B.
   The solid in Box D has 2 faces.
   The solid in Box A has no faces.

   Box A: _____   Box B: _____

   Box C: _____   Box D: _____

3. Hidden figures: square, rhombus, circle, rectangle
   The figures in Boxes C and D have all sides equal.
   The figure in Box B is not a polygon.
   The figures in Boxes A and C have right angles.

   Box A: _____   Box B: _____

   Box C: _____   Box D: _____

© Pearson Education, Inc. 4

Name _____

Symbol Acrobatics

You can write words or phrases by using symbols. For example, if you drew a picture of a bee, it could stand for the word "be." In the exercises below, each symbol stands for a word or a syllable. Before you can solve the exercise, you must first flip, slide, or turn each symbol. Write the word or phrase for each exercise.

1.   _____

2.   _____

3.   _____

4. the   _____

5. the _____

© Pearson Education, Inc. 4

Name_____

Let It Snow!

Snow crystals usually form as 6-sided stars, but are different in detailed appearance.

1. Draw all lines of symmetry on the snow crystal to the right.

2. Draw your own snow crystal design. Make sure it has symmetry.

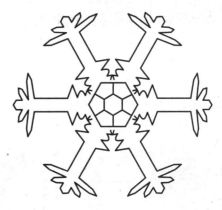

3. Draw your own snow crystal design, but this time make sure it has NO symmetry.

4. Decide which design you like best. Explain why you chose that design. Give specific reasons.

_____

_____

_____

_____

© Pearson Education, Inc. 4

Similarity

Circle the similar figures in each set.

1.

2.

3.

4.

5.

6.

7.

8.

9.

10.

© Pearson Education, Inc. 4

Poly Shapes

Each figure is made of at least 2 polygons. Draw a line or lines to show the figures. Name each figure. Be specific.

1.  _____

_____

2. 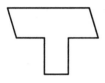 _____

_____

3. _____

_____

4. _____

_____

5. _____

_____

6. _____

_____

© Pearson Education, Inc. 4

All the Way Around

For each exercise, complete the figure by drawing a polygon with the perimeter shown. Write the length of each side of your polygon.

1.
2 | 3   P = 10

2.
4 / 5   P = 11

3.
3 / 6   P = 18

4.
3 | 3 | 3   P = 14

5.
2 \ 2 / 2   P = 12

6.
5 \ 5 / 4   P = 21

7.
4 \ 4 / 4   P = 20

8.
3 / 6   P = 22

9.
3 3 3 3 3 3   P = 24

10.
5   P = 30

11.
10 / 10   P = 30

© Pearson Education, Inc. 4

Name_____

Fair Enough

Carl is scheduling students to work at the school fair. Each student will work a 2 hr shift. The students who have signed up to work are Anna, Byron, Carlos, Donald, Esha, Frank, Glynis, Hannah, and Juan.

In each exercise fill out a schedule for student workers that meets the requirements stated.

1. Anna and Juan cannot work on Wednesday. Donald can work only on Thursday. Carlos can work only the last shift.

	Wednesday	Thursday	Friday
10 A.M.–noon			
noon–2 P.M.			
2 P.M.–4 P.M.			

2. Esha cannot work on Friday. Hannah can work only in the morning. Frank and Glynis are only available on Wednesday and Thursday.

	Wednesday	Thursday	Friday
10 A.M.–noon			
noon–2 P.M.			
2 P.M.–4 P.M.			

3. Carlos can work either Wednesday or Friday. Byron is available only from 10:00 A.M. to noon on Thursday. Juan cannot work the last shift.

	Wednesday	Thursday	Friday
10 A.M.–noon			
noon–2 P.M.			
2 P.M.–4 P.M.			

© Pearson Education, Inc. 4

Name ______________________________

Perimeter Patterns

E 8-12
VISUAL THINKING

Draw the next figure in each pattern. Find the perimeter in units for each figure.

1.

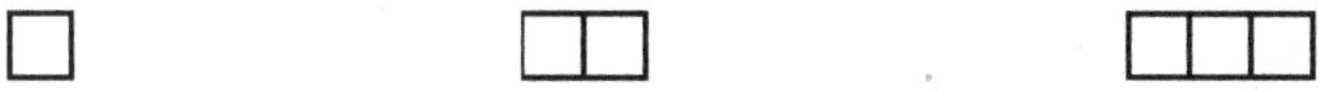

p = ______ p = ______ p = ______ p = ______

2.

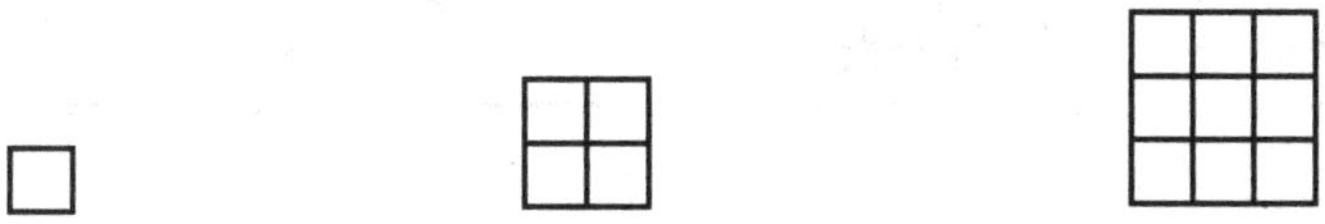

p = ______ p = ______ p = ______ p = ______

3.

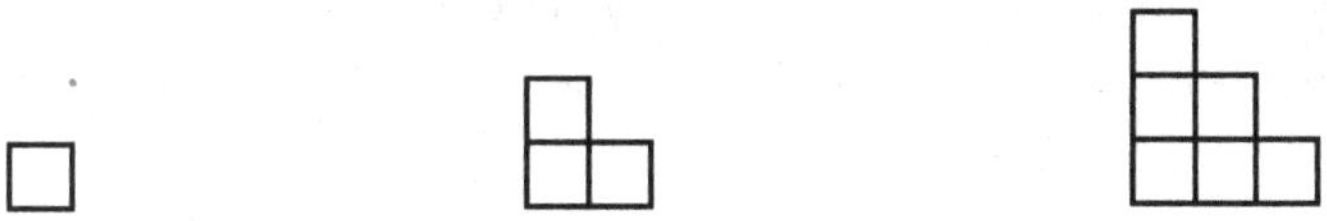

p = ______ p = ______ p = ______ p = ______

4. What pattern do you see in the perimeters for the figures in

a. Exercise 1? ______________________

b. Exercise 2? ______________________

c. Exercise 3? ______________________

5. If the patterns in Exercises 1–3 continue, what will the perimeters of each of the fifth figures be? Draw each fifth figure to check.

______, ______, ______

© Pearson Education, Inc. 4

Building Blocks

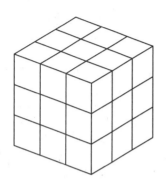

1. What is the volume of this shape in cubic units? _____

2. On how many cubes do you see 3 faces? _____

3. On how many cubes do you see 2 faces? _____

4. How many show only 1 face? _____

5. How many are hidden from view? _____

6. Write a number sentence using the answers from Exercises 1–4 to find the answer to Exercise 5.

_____

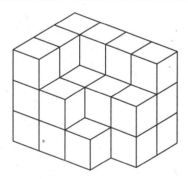

7. On how many cubes do you see 3 faces? _____

8. On how many cubes do you see 2 faces? _____

9. How many show only 1 face? _____

10. How many cubes are hidden from view? _____

11. What is the volume of this shape in cubic units? _____

© Pearson Education, Inc. 4

Applause

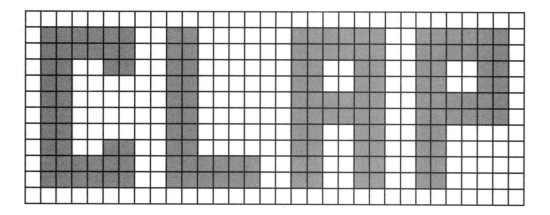

1. Complete the table below by writing the perimeters and areas of the block letters. (Hint: You can break the areas into smaller parts.)

Letter	Perimeter	Area
C		
L		
A		
P		

2. Draw your initials in block letters on the grid below and find the perimeter and area of each letter.

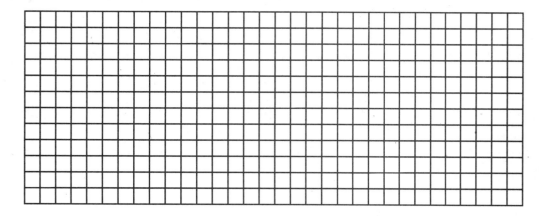

© Pearson Education, Inc. 4

Match Maker

Match the figure on the left with the figure on the right that shows an equal amount shaded.

1. 　　　　　

2. 　　　　　

© Pearson Education, Inc. 4

Look Alikes

Write the fraction from the box that shows the smaller part of each group. You will not use all of the fractions.

Fraction Box		$\frac{3}{4}$	$\frac{3}{7}$	$\frac{1}{4}$
$\frac{3}{8}$	$\frac{5}{8}$	$\frac{1}{3}$	$\frac{3}{5}$	$\frac{5}{6}$
$\frac{1}{6}$	$\frac{2}{3}$	$\frac{4}{7}$	$\frac{2}{5}$

1. _____

2. _____

3. _____

4. _____

5. _____

6. _____

© Pearson Education, Inc. 4

Name_____

Paper Fun

E 9-3
NUMBER SENSE

Read the steps in the box. Then answer the questions.

Step 1: Tyler and Ashley each have a rectangular sheet of paper.

Step 2: Tyler folds his paper in half and Ashley folds her paper into three equal parts.

Step 3: Tyler and Ashley open their papers and label the creased lines with a fraction that represents the length of the paper at the creased line.

Step 4: Tyler and Ashley refold the paper as in step 2.

Step 5: Tyler folds his paper into three equal parts and Ashley folds her paper into two equal parts.

Step 6: Tyler and Ashley open their papers and label the creased lines with fractions that represent the length of the paper at each creased line.

---

1. What fraction did Tyler and Ashley write on the creased line of their papers in step 3?

   _____

2. What fractions did Tyler and Ashley write on the creased lines of their papers in step 6?

   _____

3. Are there any creases on Ashley's paper that are labeled differently than those on Tyler's paper? What are they?

   _____

4. Are there any creases on Tyler's paper that are labeled differently than those on Ashley's paper? What are they?

   _____

© Pearson Education, Inc. 4

112 Use with Lesson 9-3.

Time After Time

JANUARY

S	M	T	W	T	F	S
		1	2	3	4	5
6	7	8	9	10	11	12
13	14	15	16	17	18	19
20	21	22	23	24	25	26
27	28	29	30	31		

APRIL

S	M	T	W	T	F	S
	1	2	3	4	5	6
7	8	9	10	11	12	13
14	15	16	17	18	19	20
21	22	23	24	25	26	27
28	29	30				

JULY

S	M	T	W	T	F	S
	1	2	3	4	5	6
7	8	9	10	11	12	13
14	15	16	17	18	19	20
21	22	23	24	25	26	27
28	29	30	31			

OCTOBER

S	M	T	W	T	F	S
	1	2	3	4	5	
6	7	8	9	10	11	12
13	14	15	16	17	18	19
20	21	22	23	24	25	26
27	28	29	30	31		

Estimate the fraction of each month that passed before the date given.

1. January 8 _____

2. October 17 _____

3. April 16 _____

4. July 5 _____

5. October 10 _____

6. January 25 _____

7. July 6 _____

8. April 30 _____

© Pearson Education, Inc. 4

Picture Patterns

Use the pictures to find the pattern. Then complete the table.

1.

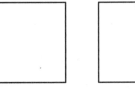

| Square piece of paper | 1 fold | 2 folds | 3 folds | 4 folds | 5 folds |

Number of folds	1	2	3	4	5
Number of parts	2	4	8		
Fraction for one part	$\frac{1}{2}$	$\frac{1}{4}$	$\frac{1}{8}$		

2.

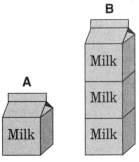

Carton stack	A	B	C	D	E
Number of cartons	1	3			
Fraction for one carton	1	$\frac{1}{3}$			

3.

A B C

Figure	A	B	C	D	E
Number of squares	2				
Fraction of shaded squares	$\frac{1}{2}$				

© Pearson Education, Inc. 4

It's a Draw!

Shade the diagram at the right to show a fraction that is equivalent to the fraction of shaded squares shown by the diagram at the left. Then write the equivalent fraction.

1.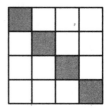

_____

2.

_____

3.

_____

4.

_____

5.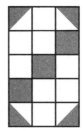

_____

6.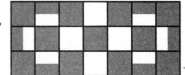

_____

© Pearson Education, Inc. 4

Matching Money

Match the amount of the coins shown in Column 1 with the
dollar amounts in Column 2 and the fractions in Column 3.

1.

A $0.80   **I** $\frac{3}{10}$

2.

B $0.50   **II** $\frac{4}{5}$

3.

C $0.25   **III** $\frac{9}{10}$

4.

D $0.07   **IV** $\frac{3}{4}$

5.

E $0.90   **V** $\frac{7}{100}$

6.

F $0.75   **VI** $\frac{1}{4}$

7.

G $0.30   **VII** $\frac{1}{2}$

© Pearson Education, Inc. 4

Name_____

Comparing Outcomes

Tiffany tossed a number cube 12 times. Then she made a tally chart to show each time the cube showed each face.

Face	1	2	3	4	5	6
Number	I	III	II		II	IIII

1. Complete the table to show the fraction of tosses for each face of the number cube.

Face	1	2	3	4	5	6
Fraction (out of 12 tosses)	$\frac{1}{12}$					

2. Compare the fractional results for each face by writing >, <, or = in each ☐.

   A. Face 1 ☐ Face 2   **B.** Face 3 ☐ Face 5

   C. Face 5 ☐ Face 4   **D.** Face 2 ☐ Face 6

Tiffany tossed a coin 10 times and had 6 heads and 4 tails.
Then she tossed a coin 20 times and had 8 heads and 12 tails.

3. Complete the table to show the fractions of heads and tails Tiffany tossed.

Outcome	Heads	Tails
Fraction out of 10		
Fraction out of 20		

4. Compare the fractional results for each set of tosses by writing >, <, or = in each ☐.

   A. heads out of 10 ☐ tails out of 10

   B. heads out of 20 ☐ tails out of 20

   C. heads out of 10 ☐ heads out of 20

   D. heads out of 10 ☐ tails out of 20

© Pearson Education, Inc. 4

Triangle Fractions

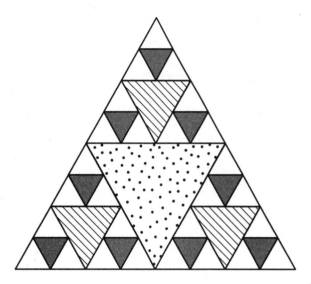

1. What fraction of a striped triangle is a shaded triangle? What fraction of the spotted triangle is a shaded triangle? Use >, <, or = to compare the two fractions.

    _____

2. What fraction of the spotted triangle is a white triangle? What fraction of a striped triangle is three shaded triangles? Use >, <, or = to compare the two fractions.

    _____

3. What fraction of the spotted triangle is two striped triangles? What fraction of the largest triangle is one spotted triangle? Use >, <, or = to compare the two fractions.

    _____

4. What fraction of the largest triangle is one striped triangle? What fraction of the largest triangle is four shaded triangles? Use >, <, or = to compare the two fractions.

    _____

© Pearson Education, Inc. 4

Name_____

Recreation Time!

1. Timothy has computer class 3 times a week. Each class is 45 min long. How many hours of computer class does Timothy have per week? In 4 weeks?

   _____

2. Alex practices soccer 4 times a week for 50 min each practice. How many total hours does Alex practice soccer per week? In 2 weeks?

   _____

3. Laurel went swimming 7 times in 3 weeks. One time she swam for $1\frac{1}{2}$ hr. The other 6 times she swam for 30 min each time. How many hours did Laurel swim in 3 weeks?

   _____

4. Caitlin, Cindy, and Connie went jogging at the recreation center. Caitlin jogged for 40 min, Cindy jogged for 30 min, and Connie jogged for 70 min. What was the total amount of time they jogged altogether?

   _____

5. Dena takes karate classes every Tuesday and Thursday. Each class is 55 min long. How many hours of class will Dena have in 3 weeks?

   _____

6. Jack spent $9\frac{3}{4}$ hr practicing ice hockey with his team. How many $\frac{1}{4}$ hr is that?

   _____

7. Misa takes 3 dance classes each week. Ballet class is 45 min long, modern dance is 50 min long, and jazz dance is 35 min long. How many hours of dance class does Misa have in 2 weeks?

   _____

8. Carlos practices piano every Monday, Wednesday, and Friday for 35 min each day. He also practices guitar every Tuesday, Thursday, and Saturday for 30 min each day. How many hours does Carlos spend practicing musical instruments each week?

   _____

© Pearson Education, Inc. 4

Name_____

Stamping Fractions

Sheet = 20 stamps

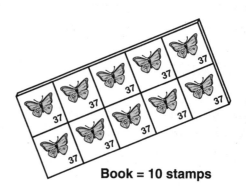

Book = 10 stamps

Use the pictures of the stamps to answer the questions.

1. Which is a greater number of stamps, $2\frac{3}{10}$ books of stamps or $1\frac{1}{20}$ sheets of stamps?

   _____

2. Would you rather have $2\frac{1}{10}$ sheets of stamps or $3\frac{9}{10}$ books of stamps?

   _____

3. Brandon used $\frac{28}{10}$ books of stamps, and Lindsey used $1\frac{3}{4}$ sheets of stamps. Who used more stamps?

   _____

4. Thomas has $3\frac{1}{5}$ books of stamps, and Ron has 28 stamps. Who has more stamps?

   _____

5. The stamps in the sheet and book shown above cost the same amount per stamp. Which costs more, $2\frac{3}{20}$ sheets or $4\frac{2}{5}$ books?

   _____

6. Scott bought 2 books of stamps and 1 sheet of stamps. He used three stamps each day for 3 days. How many books of stamps did Scott have left after 3 days?

   _____

© Pearson Education, Inc. 4

Circles and Rectangles

Complete each statement by writing the letter of the picture that shows the equivalent fraction.

1. 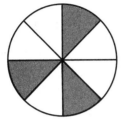 is the same fraction as _____.

A.

B.

C.

2. 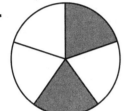 is the same fraction as _____.

A.

B.

C.

3. 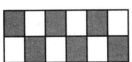 is the same fraction as _____.

A.   **B.**
   or

4. 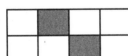 is the same fraction as _____.

A.   **B.**
   or

5. 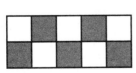 is the same fraction as _____.

A.   **B.**
   or

© Pearson Education, Inc. 4

Name_____

Shape Fractions

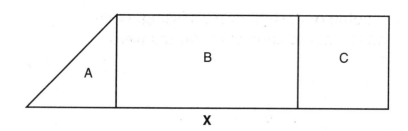

1. What fraction of trapezoid X is square C? Explain your answer.

_____

_____

2. What fraction of trapezoid X is rectangle B? Explain your answer.

_____

_____

3. What fraction of trapezoid X is triangle A? Explain your answer.

_____

_____

4. What fraction of shape Z is square J?
Explain your answer.

_____

_____

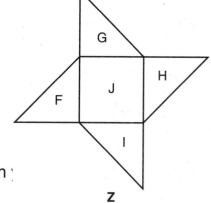

5. What fraction of shape Z is triangle G? Explain '

_____

_____

© Pearson Education, Inc. 4

Missing Information

In the list of math words, some of the letters are missing. Write the missing letters. Then tell what fraction of the letters were missing from each word.

1. Fr____ct____ons

Fraction missing: —————

2. C____ ____cle

Fraction missing: —————

3. E____ui____ale____t

Fraction missing: —————

4. Pol____g____n

Fraction missing: —————

5. Ci____cu____feren____e

Fraction missing: —————

6. Kil____g____am

Fraction missing: —————

7. Mi____ ____ilite____s

Fraction missing: —————

8. D____a____e____e____

Fraction missing: —————

© Pearson Education, Inc. 4

A Fraction of Time

Chore	Amount of Time to Complete
Sweep floor	$\frac{2}{6}$ hr
Fold clothes	$\frac{1}{5}$ hr
Dust	$\frac{4}{6}$ hr
Wash windows	$\frac{5}{8}$ hr
Cut grass	$\frac{2}{3}$ hr
Weed garden	$\frac{3}{4}$ hr
Feed pets	$\frac{1}{8}$ hr

Ken has 1 hr to complete some chores around the house.
Estimate to decide whether the 2 chores listed could be
completed within 1 hr. Use < or > for each ◯.

1. sweep floor and fold clothes ◯ hour

2. weed garden and wash windows ◯ hour

3. fold clothes and cut grass ◯ hour

4. feed pets and fold clothes ◯ hour

5. cut grass and weed garden ◯ hour

6. Which combination of 2 chores can be completed in
exactly 1 hr?

_____

_____

7. If Ken had to feed the pets, what other chore could he do
to complete both chores in 1 hr or less?

_____

© Pearson Education, Inc. 4

Number Search

Circle the fraction pairs that have a sum greater than 1. Pairs can be made across or up and down.

1.

$\frac{4}{6}$	$\frac{2}{6}$	$\frac{1}{6}$	$\frac{5}{6}$
$\frac{4}{6}$	$\frac{2}{6}$	$\frac{4}{6}$	$\frac{3}{6}$
$\frac{3}{6}$	$\frac{5}{6}$	$\frac{2}{6}$	$\frac{1}{6}$
$\frac{3}{6}$	$\frac{1}{6}$	$\frac{5}{6}$	$\frac{4}{6}$

2. What is the sum of all the fractions not circled in Exercise 1?

_____

3.

$\frac{1}{8}$	$\frac{4}{8}$	$\frac{7}{8}$	$\frac{2}{8}$
$\frac{3}{8}$	$\frac{5}{8}$	$\frac{3}{8}$	$\frac{1}{8}$
$\frac{6}{8}$	$\frac{1}{8}$	$\frac{4}{8}$	$\frac{5}{8}$
$\frac{5}{8}$	$\frac{2}{8}$	$\frac{6}{8}$	$\frac{2}{8}$

4. What is the sum of all the fractions not circled in Exercise 3?

_____

© Pearson Education, Inc. 4

Name_____

Bar None

Mrs. Howard had health bars for her students to eat during their
snack time. The bars were each divided into an equal number of
parts. Use the pictures of the bars to find how much each
student ate.

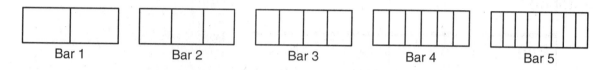

Bar 1   Bar 2   Bar 3   Bar 4   Bar 5

1. Maria ate one piece of Bar 1 and two pieces of Bar 2. Draw
   a picture that represents what Maria ate.

2. Barb ate one piece of Bar 2 and two pieces of Bar 3. Write
   an addition sentence to find out how much she ate.

   _____

3. Mark ate one piece of Bar 1 and four pieces of Bar 5. Write
   an addition sentence to find how much he ate.

   _____

4. Kerry ate two pieces of Bar 5 and three pieces of Bar 4.
   Write an addition sentence to find how much she ate.

   _____

5. How much is left? Explain how you know.

   _____

   _____

© Pearson Education, Inc. 4

Book Plan

The students in Mr. Martin's class are writing their autobiographies. The shaded table shows Ed's plan for his story. Complete the fraction chart for Ed's autobiography.

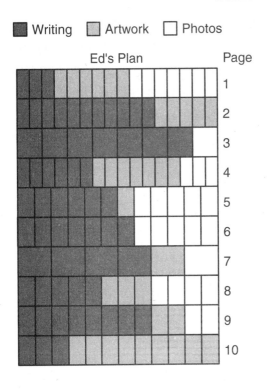

Writing Artwork Photos

Ed's Plan   Page

Page	Writing	Artwork	Photos
1.		$\frac{6}{16}$	
2.	$\frac{11}{16}$		
3.			$\frac{1}{8}$
4.	$\frac{6}{16}$		
5.		$\frac{1}{12}$	
6.			$\frac{5}{12}$
7.		$\frac{1}{6}$	
8.			$\frac{4}{12}$
9.		$\frac{2}{12}$	
10.	$\frac{3}{12}$		

11. Ed designed one page by drawing a family tree and including photos of 3 generations of his family. Which page do you think best represents his family tree?

_____

12. Ed designed one page that told the story of his lost pet with a photo of "Dubie." Which page do you think best represents this information?

_____

© Pearson Education, Inc. 4

Name_____

Fraction Subtraction

Three of the fractions in each of the exercises below make a subtraction sentence. Work from left to right. Write a minus sign and an equal sign between the 3 fractions to make each subtraction sentence. Then circle each completed subtraction sentence. The first one has been done for you.

1. $\frac{1}{2}$ $\left(\frac{3}{4} - \frac{1}{8} = \frac{5}{8}\right)$ $\frac{7}{8}$ $\frac{1}{4}$

2. $\frac{1}{3}$ $\frac{4}{5}$ $\frac{5}{6}$ $\frac{2}{3}$ $\frac{1}{6}$ $\frac{5}{12}$

3. $\frac{7}{10}$ $\frac{3}{5}$ $\frac{5}{6}$ $\frac{4}{5}$ $\frac{1}{2}$ $\frac{3}{10}$

4. $\frac{2}{5}$ $\frac{3}{5}$ $\frac{1}{3}$ $\frac{4}{15}$ $\frac{4}{5}$ $\frac{7}{15}$

5. $\frac{7}{12}$ $\frac{1}{4}$ $\frac{1}{3}$ $\frac{2}{3}$ $\frac{10}{12}$ $\frac{3}{4}$

6. $\frac{3}{20}$ $\frac{7}{10}$ $\frac{9}{20}$ $\frac{1}{10}$ $\frac{7}{20}$ $\frac{9}{20}$

7. $\frac{1}{6}$ $\frac{6}{7}$ $\frac{1}{2}$ $\frac{5}{14}$ $\frac{3}{7}$ $\frac{5}{14}$

8. $\frac{8}{9}$ $\frac{8}{27}$ $\frac{16}{27}$ $\frac{1}{9}$ $\frac{7}{18}$ $\frac{2}{9}$

9. Subtract across and down to complete the fraction square.

$\frac{7}{8}$	$\frac{1}{4}$	
$\frac{1}{3}$	$\frac{1}{8}$	

© Pearson Education, Inc. 4

Pet Problem

Brian, Anna, and Karen each own a pet. Use the facts below to fill in the charts. Write yes or no in the columns as you gather information.

Color

	White	Tan	Brown
Angie			
Brian			
Karen			

Pet

	Hamster	Cat	Dog

- Angie has a pet that is tan.

- Brian does not have a dog.

- Angie's best friend is Karen.

- Brian lives next door to Angie.

- Angie's best friend's pet is a white hamster.

- Brian's next door neighbor has a dog.

- Someone has a brown cat.

1. What color pet does each child have?

_____

_____

_____

© Pearson Education, Inc. 4

Proportional Drawing

Enlarge the picture by graphing ordered pairs. To start, find the coordinates of the vertices of the cube on the smaller grid and plot them on the larger grid. Then connect the points.

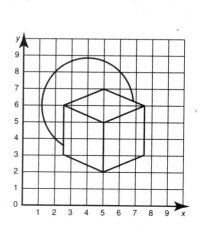

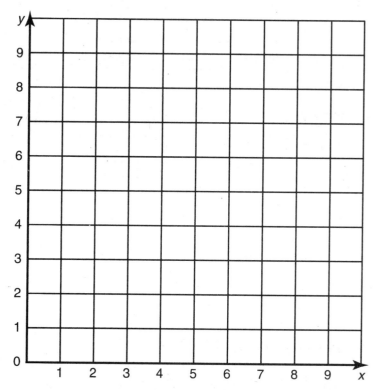

1. What does a side of the small cube measure in inches?

_____

2. What does the side of the larger cube measure in inches?

_____

_____

© Pearson Education, Inc. 4

Name_____

A New Measure

Distance *AB* is a new measurement called a pflugel.

Write the fractional part of a pflugel.

1. Distance *DB* _____

2. Distance *AE* _____

3. Distance *EC* _____

4. Distance *GB* _____

5. Distance *AG* _____

6. What is the total of *AC* + *DB*? _____

7. $1\frac{1}{4}$ pflugel = *CB* + *AF* + _____

8. $1\frac{1}{2}$ pflugel = *AC* + *BC* + *AG* + _____

© Pearson Education, Inc. 4

Name_____

Label the Containers

Match each description to the container whose capacity best measures it.

_____ _____ _____ _____ _____ _____

_____ _____ _____ _____ _____ _____

a. testing soup to see if it is too hot

b. milk for school lunch

c. measure of nuts for health bar mix

d. enough milk for family of four for a day

e. 6 to 8 of these filled with water a day for good health

f. enough milk for breakfast cereal for one day for your family

g. container of dog food for a week

h. enough fruit preserves to put on toast

© Pearson Education, Inc. 4

A Day in the Park

James, Mary, Chris, and Brooke want to see who lives the closest to the park. Use the information below to make a bar graph. Then use the graph to answer the questions.

a. Mary lives 6 blocks from the park.

b. Chris lives 3 blocks closer to the park than Mary does.

c. Brooke lives 5 blocks farther from the park than Chris.

d. James lives half as far from the park as Brooke does.

1. Who lives the closest to the park? _____

2. Who lives farthest from the park? _____

3. Who lives twice as far from the park as Chris? _____

© Pearson Education, Inc. 4

Name _____

Can you Substitute?

Janice is at the grocery store buying items to do her cooking for the week.

1. Janice needs 1 pt of sour cream. Which container should she buy, and how many of them does she need to purchase?

_____

_____

_____

2. Janice needs 16 oz of tomato juice. Which container should she buy, and how many of them does she need to purchase?

_____

_____

_____

3. Janice needs 4 c of skim milk. Which container should she buy, and how many of them does she need to purchase?

_____

_____

_____

4. Janice needs 32 oz of sugar. Which container should she buy, and how many of them does she need to purchase?

_____

_____

_____

© Pearson Education, Inc. 4

Find a Pair

The following list has six pairs of partial products that can be combined to form one multiplication problem. For example, **a** and **j** can be combined to make one problem as follows:

j. + **a.**

$(12 \times 40) + (12 \times 3) =$

$12 \times (40 + 3) =$

12×43

Match the five remaining pairs. List each pair and combine the pairs into a single problem as shown above.

a. 12×3	**b.** 72×10	**c.** 47×2	**d.** 39×20
e. 97×50	**f.** 61×10	**g.** 47×30	**h.** 39×4
i. 72×6	**j.** 12×40	**k.** 97×2	**l.** 61×5

1. _____

_____

2. _____

_____

3. _____

_____

4. _____

_____

5. _____

_____

© Pearson Education, Inc. 4

Who Has What?

1. Ken, Paul, and Karen each have $0.50. Ken has 6 coins, Paul also has 6 coins but not the same coins as Ken, and Karen has 7 coins. What coins does each one have?

_____

_____

_____

2. Ken, Paul, and Karen each have $0.75. Ken has 7 coins, Paul also has 7 coins but not the same coins as Ken, and Karen has 8 coins. What coins does each one have?

_____

_____

_____

3. Ken, Paul, and Karen each have $1.35. Ken has 11 coins, Paul has 10 coins, and Karen has 8 coins. What coins does each one have?

_____

_____

_____

4. John buys a toy that costs $4.49. He gives the clerk $5.00. He gets 3 coins in change. What coins does he receive?

_____

5. Hank buys a new CD for $9.99 and a pack of batteries for $5.39. He gives the clerk $20.00. He receives 4 bills and 9 coins in change. What bills and coins does he receive?

_____

© Pearson Education, Inc. 4

Name_____

Riddle

Solve the riddles by choosing the letter of the value that is different in each group.

It has been said that a person who runs behind a car gets

_____ .

1. **T** $\frac{1}{4}$ **E** 2.5   **L** $\frac{25}{100}$ **R** 0.25   _____

2. **C** 2.14   **R** $2\frac{7}{50}$ **X** $2\frac{14}{10}$ **I** $\frac{107}{50}$ _____

3. **R** 0.50   **H** $\frac{5}{100}$ **M** $\frac{1}{2}$ **E** $\frac{3}{6}$ _____

4. **A** 0.08   **E** $\frac{4}{10}$ **D** 0.40   **H** $\frac{2}{5}$ _____

5. **W** $\frac{41}{10}$ **D** $4\frac{1}{10}$ **U** 4.01   **M** 4.10   _____

6. **S** 0.3   **T** $\frac{10}{100}$ **D** 0.1   **E** $\frac{3}{30}$ _____

7. **L** $\frac{12}{16}$ **T** $\frac{3}{8}$ **I** 0.75   **C** $\frac{75}{100}$ _____

8. **A** $1\frac{1}{2}$ **E** 0.15   **I** 1.5   **O** $\frac{6}{4}$ _____

9. **D** 0.4   **N** $\frac{5}{20}$ **S** 0.25   **R** $\frac{25}{100}$ _____

It has also been said that the person who runs in front of a car gets

_____ .

10. **T** 0.06   **L** $\frac{3}{5}$ **S** 0.60   **R** $\frac{60}{100}$ _____

11. **A** $\frac{3}{25}$ **I** 0.75   **O** 0.12   **T** $\frac{12}{100}$ _____

12. **D** 1.75   **R** $\frac{9}{4}$ **E** $1\frac{75}{100}$ **M** $1\frac{3}{4}$ _____

13. **E** 0.20   **N** $\frac{1}{50}$ **C** 0.02   **K** $\frac{2}{100}$ _____

14. **S** 4.8   **L** $4\frac{4}{5}$ **S** $4\frac{8}{10}$ **D** 4.40   _____

© Pearson Education, Inc. 4

Triangular Connections

Draw a triangle connecting the standard form, word form, and expanded form of each number. As an example, points *A, G,* and *M* have been connected for you.

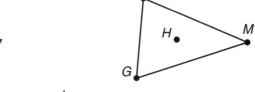

A. 1.16

B. Three and seven tenths

C. 16 + 0.1 + 0.06

D. 1.6

E. 3.7

F. 3 + 0.07

G. One and sixteen hundredths

H. 3.07

I. Sixteen and sixteen hundredths

J. 1 + 0.6

K. 3 + 0.7

L. One and six tenths

M. 1 + 0.1 + 0.06

N. 16.16

O. Three and seven hundredths

© Pearson Education, Inc. 4

Do We Decimal?

In many libraries, nonfiction books are placed on shelves in order according to the Dewey Decimal System.

Help the librarian decide where to put the list of books that have been returned. Write the abbreviation for the section where each returned book should be placed. Then write the exact place where each book should be shelved. The first book has been done for you.

| 003.1 | 027.4 | 029.9 | 038.1 | 042.1 | 042.9 | 047.01 | 051.1 | 056.12 | 057.1 | 057.19 | 058.7 |
General (G)

| 102.2 | 107.31 | 116.09 | 122.05 | 122.96 | 147.3 | 151.61 | 151.9 | 152.09 | 153.6 |
Philosophy & Psychology (PP)

| 510.10 | 516.05 | 521.3 | 550.11 | 551.62 | 563.07 | 572.1 | 574.73 | 581.71 | 586.8 | 587.09 | 587.22 | 591.6 |
Sciences & Mathematics (SM)

| 808.1 | 812.4 | 813.21 | 856.65 | 881.9 | 882.4 | 886.89 |
Literature (L)

1. 109.7   PP; Between 107.31 and 116.09 _____

2. 152.08 _____

3. 042.13 _____

4. 006.8 _____

5. 503.54 _____

6. 550.06 _____

7. 813.12 _____

8. 107.05 _____

9. 886.9 _____

10. 057.01 _____

11. 587.21 _____

12. 122.5 _____

© Pearson Education, Inc. 4

What Doesn't Fit?

Find and circle the item that does not belong in each group.

1.

2.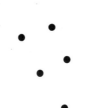

3.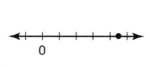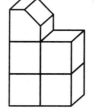

4.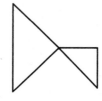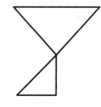

5.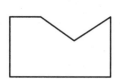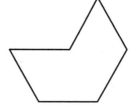

6.

© Pearson Education, Inc. 4

Name_____

Shopping Swap

Four friends went shopping to buy presents for their families. Each started with the same amount of money, $20.00. Somehow, the shopping bags got all mixed up by the end of the shopping trip. Use estimation to place the name of the shopper under his or her correct bag.

- April has $13.43 left.
- Carole has $0.16 left.
- Victor has $7.19 left.
- Zoe has $11.04 left.

1.

$3.67 $16.17

_____

2.

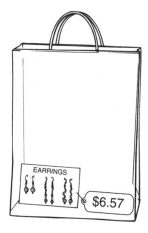

EARRINGS $6.57

_____

3.

$1.49   PEN PAK $7.47

_____

4.

$12.81

_____

© Pearson Education, Inc. 4

Name_____

Pascal's Triangle

A famous mathematician named Pascal invented a triangle with many different patterns. Here is his triangle using decimals. Fill in the missing numbers.

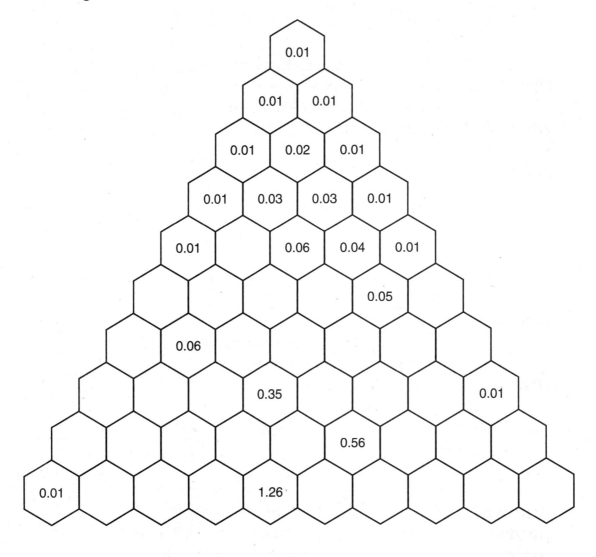

1. What are some patterns you found in the triangle?

_____

_____

_____

© Pearson Education, Inc. 4

Space Vacation

The Decima family is from the planet Meteria. They are trying to make some choices for their family vacation. Help them decide.

1. Choices: Leteria or Megorite

Facts: Leteria is 2.7 deca-years from home.

Megorite is 1.9 deca-years from home.

The family has 6.2 deca-years for vacation.

Other factors: Leteria has theme park and water sports.

Megorite has theme park and skiing.

What planet should they visit? Why?

_____

_____

2. Choices: Ultra pak, Standard pak, or Budget pak

Cost: 3.5 zerbs   2.9 zerbs   1.2 zerbs

Facts: budget = 30 zerbs   need = 10 paks

Other factors: Ultra includes variety, nutrition, and is tasty.

Standard includes nutrition and is tasty.

Budget includes adequate nutrition.

What food should they buy? Why?

_____

_____

3. Grammit Decima would like to buy some gifts for his grandparents with his 16 zerbs. He wants either a hat or a belt for his grandfather and a picture or a blanket for his grandmother. A hat is 5.7 zerbs, a belt is 9.3 zerbs, a picture is 8.6 zerbs, and a blanket is 6.1 zerbs. What should Grammit buy and why?

_____

_____

_____

© Pearson Education, Inc. 4

Whole Pieces

In each of the following, look at the figure on the left, then find
and circle 2 figures on the right that can be combined to form
the first figure. The partial figures may be turned, but not flipped.

1.

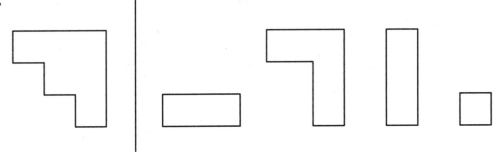

2.

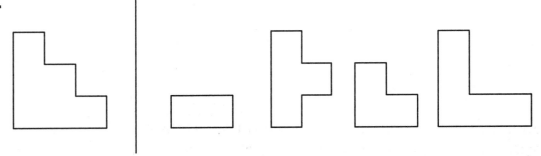

3.

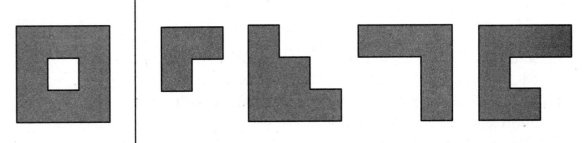

4.

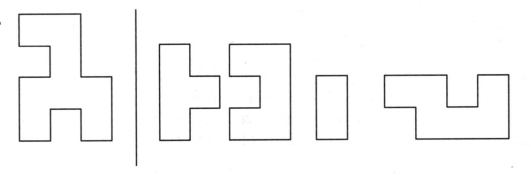

© Pearson Education, Inc. 4

Name_____

My Aunt's a Doll!

Sarah is having a very special porcelain doll made for her favorite aunt. The doll is going to be 1 m tall, and she wants it to look as realistic as possible. Sarah's aunt is 5 ft 6 in. tall.

1. About how many centimeters long should the legs be? Explain how you decided.

_____

_____

_____

2. The doll's head is 18 cm long. The choices for the eyes are 1 mm, 2 cm, and 5 cm in diameter. Which eye choice should Sarah pick for the doll?

_____

3. Sarah's aunt has long, wavy, brown hair that reaches halfway down her back. It is about 22 in. long. About how long should the doll's hair be?

_____

4. After the doll was completed, Sarah received an itemized bill. The price of the doll's hat was based on a hat that measured 50 cm in diameter. Do you think this item has been listed correctly? Explain.

_____

_____

5. Sarah gave the doll to Aunt Jane on her birthday. Sarah knows that Aunt Jane was born 3 years after Sarah's mother, and that Sarah's mother is 24 years older than Sarah is. Sarah is 9 years old. How old is Aunt Jane?

_____

© Pearson Education, Inc. 4

Clever Scientists

Jane and Jim are in Mr. Marten's science class. They have been chosen to make the fruit smoothie that will be served at the student council breakfast. They need to make 3 L of the drink but the only measuring devices left in the science lab are the following.

5 mL beaker   20 mL beaker   500 mL beaker

Explain how they can use the three beakers to measure out the following ingredients.

1. One half of a liter of raspberry juice

_____

2. 750 mL of blueberry juice

_____

_____

_____

3. 1 L of sparkling water

_____

4. 460 mL of apple juice

_____

_____

_____

5. The remainder of the 3 L is crushed ice.

_____

_____

© Pearson Education, Inc. 4

Name_____

Balance the Pans

Use gram measures—1 g, 3 g, and 9 g—to balance each pan. The left column in the chart shows the mass of the object that is on the left pan to start with. Fill in the middle and right columns with the mass you would add to both sides to balance the pans. The first one has been done for you.

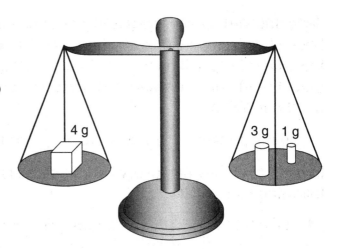

	Mass of Object on Left Pan	Mass Added to Left Pan	Mass Added to Right Pan
1.	1 g	0	1 g
2.	3 g		
3.	5 g		
4.	8 g		
5.	9 g		
6.	10 g		
7.	12 g		
8.	15 g		

© Pearson Education, Inc. 4

Crossmath Puzzle

Fill in each square of the crossword puzzle using metric unit numbers.

ACROSS

1. 6 L 140 mL = ___ mL

3. 3 m 4 cm = ___ mm

5. 5 m = ___ cm

7. 7 kg = ___ g

9. 1 km 400 m = ___ m

10. 4 kg 20 g = ___ g

11. 9 L 30 mL = ___ mL

13. 8 m 6 dm = ___ cm

15. 70 m 40 cm = ___ cm

16. 625 cm = ___ mm

17. 13 L = ___ mL

DOWN

1. ___ g = 6 kg

2. 4,000 dm 200 cm = ___ m

3. 30 kg = ___ g

4. ___ m = 2 km 20 m

6. 8,100 mm = ___ cm

7. 7 m 1 dm = ___ cm

8. ___ mL = 2 L

12. 3 m = ___ cm

13. 80,000 g = ___ kg

14. 3,100 cm = ___ dm

15. ___ cm = 7 m 1 cm

16. 60,000 mL = ___ L

© Pearson Education, Inc. 4

Name_____

Paper By the Pound

Ashland County keeps records of the paper brought to its
recycling center. Look at the graph and answer the questions.

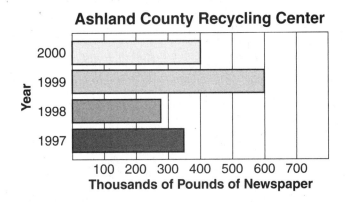

Ashland County Recycling Center

Year: 2000, 1999, 1998, 1997

100 200 300 400 500 600 700
Thousands of Pounds of Newspaper

1. About how many pounds of paper were recycled each year?

   1997 _____

   1998 _____

   1999 _____

   2000 _____

2. What was the average number of pounds of paper that
   were recycled in the 4 years shown on the graph?

   _____

3. One year, Ashland County sponsored an advertising
   campaign to encourage people to recycle. In which year do
   you think the ad campaign was sponsored? Why?

   _____

   _____

4. If the amount of newspapers recycled in 2001 were to
   equal the average, how much more paper would have to
   be recycled in 2001 than in 2000?

   _____

© Pearson Education, Inc. 4

Weather Walk

Here is a comparison of the same temperatures in Fahrenheit and Celsius.

Begin at the box that says "summer picnic," and design a path to the box that says "winter vacation." You may move directly up, down, left, or right, but not diagonally. You may only use a box that has a reasonable temperature for the activity.

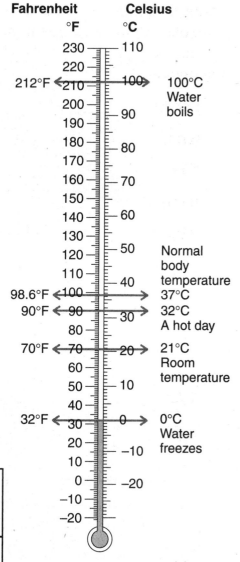

	30°C Summer picnic	84°F Swim	10°C Play baseball	−10°C Dogsled	40°C Snow-mobile
START					
	60°F Ski	20°F Ice skate	−5°C Snowball fight	70°F Beach volleyball	32°F Hang glide
	12°C Rake leaves	−40°F Surf	60°F Camping	25°F Scuba dive	65°C Mow the lawn
	84°C Water ski	−5°F Stay home	−10°C Snow board	60°F Ride bikes	20°C Ice fishing
	−15°F Gardening	84°F Bird watching	20°C Bird watching	20°C Golf	19°F Winter vacation

END

© Pearson Education, Inc. 4

Metric Mix Up!

Minnie is helping her teacher with a new bulletin board. She has completed all the pictures that illustrate measurements. But she has mixed up the labels. Help her place the labels where they belong.

Labels:

8 cm

1 m

8 mm

250 kg

320 mL

1 g

1 L

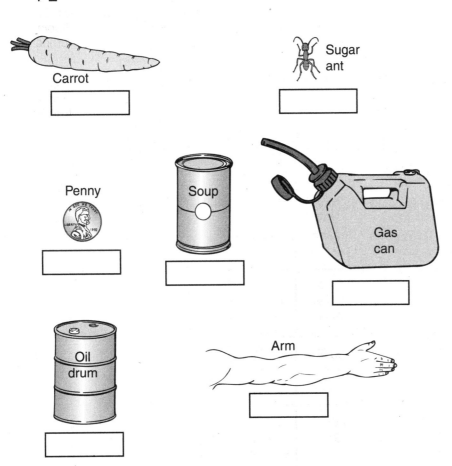

Carrot

Sugar ant

Penny

Soup

Gas can

Oil drum

Arm

© Pearson Education, Inc. 4

More or Less

Circle the numbered cubes on the right side of the inequality
symbol that make the statement true.

1.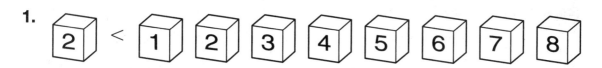

2.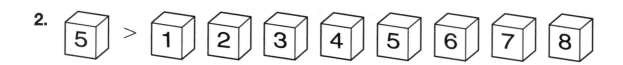

3.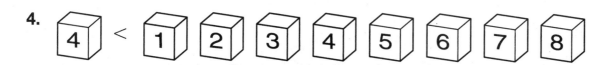

Shade the numbers on the right side of the inequality symbol
that make the statement false.

4.

5.

6.

© Pearson Education, Inc. 4

Picture Problems

Below each picture, write the number value of *n*.

1.  — *n* =

n = _____

2. *n* +  =

n = _____

3. *n* × 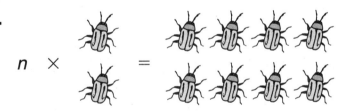 =

n = _____

4.  — *n* =

n = _____

5.  ÷ *n* =

n = _____

© Pearson Education, Inc. 4

In and Out

Each series of pictures represents the same operation that is performed on the "in" number to produce the "out" number. Answer the questions for each set of pictures.

IN   OUT   IN   OUT   IN   OUT
0   0   1   3   2   6

1. What are the out numbers from the box when the numbers 5, 10, and 20 are put in? _____

2. If x is the in number, what is the out number? _____

3. If 18 is the out number, what is the in number? _____

IN   OUT   IN   OUT   IN   OUT

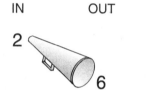  

2   6   4   10   6   14

4. What are the out numbers from the megaphone when the numbers 5, 3, and 12 are put in? _____

5. If n is the in number, what is the out number? _____

IN   OUT   IN   OUT   IN   OUT

2  4   6  36   3  9

6. What are the out numbers from the horn when the numbers 5, 7, and 4 are put in? _____

7. If numbers 64, 81, and 100 are the out numbers, what numbers were put in? _____

8. If n is the in number, what is the out number? _____

© Pearson Education, Inc. 4

Name_____

Among Friends

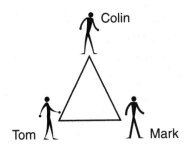

1. Colin has just won the school chess tournament. Tom and Mark congratulated Colin with high fives. Use the diagram to determine how many high fives there were if each boy gave the others a high five and there were no duplications.

_____

2. Two pairs of friends came in first and second place at a bridge tournament. Each friend gave a thumbs-up signal to the others. How many thumbs-up signals were there without any duplication among the friends?

_____

3. Five basketball players went out onto the floor and each slapped a high five to the other members.

Draw a diagram showing the possibilities.

4. How many high fives were there?   _____

5. Six people are in a circle. They start shaking hands with each other. How many handshakes are there?   _____

© Pearson Education, Inc. 4

Is It Possible?

1. Design the spinner to show that it is equally likely that a person would spin red or green but impossible that a person would spin yellow. Use R for red, G for green, and Y for yellow.

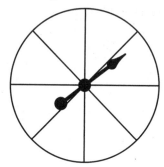

Here are the rules for a new addition game:

Row 1

- The two rows of numbered disks are turned over, and each row is mixed up within its original row.

Row 2

- The player chooses a disk from row 1 and a disk from row 2.

- The player earns a point if the sum of the two disks is equal to any of the disks in row 2.

   Example: row 1 = 1 and row 2 = 7, 1 + 7 = 8 wins a point

Is it certain or impossible to win a point for the following situations?

2. row 1 = 2 and row 2 = 6   _____

3. row 1 = 3 and row 2 = 7   _____

4. row 1 = 4 and row 2 = 7   _____

5. If a 1 is picked from row 1, which disk in row 2 would make it impossible to score a point?   _____

6. If a 5 is chosen from row 1, is it certain or impossible to score a point?   _____

© Pearson Education, Inc. 4

Triangle Shapes

Four equilateral triangles can be attached to form three different shapes by fitting two sides together as shown. (Reflections and rotations of these three shapes are not considered different shapes.)

1. Using five equilateral triangles, draw the number of different shapes possible by joining the triangles at the sides.

2. Using six equilateral triangles, show the shape of a regular hexagon that can be formed by joining the triangles at the sides.

3. Using six equilateral triangles, show a six-sided shape that is made by forming a bigger equilateral triangle and a rhombus (4 equal sides but not a square).

4. Using six equilateral triangles, show a parallelogram and three other different shapes that can be made by joining the sides.

© Pearson Education, Inc. 4

Ribbons and Socks

1. Rusty's sock drawer contains 6 loose blue socks and 6 loose red socks. One morning Rusty was not paying attention and just pulled socks from his sock drawer. How many socks should Rusty take from the drawer to be sure he has a pair? Explain your answer.

_____

2. If Rusty wants to make sure that he has a pair of blue socks, how many socks should Rusty take from the drawer? Explain your answer.

_____

3. Sarah has 8 pink ribbons, 4 blue ribbons, and 6 yellow ribbons in her ribbon drawer. How many ribbons does Sarah need to select if she wants to make sure that she has a matching pair and does not look as she pulls? Explain your answer.

_____

4. If Sarah pulled out 1 blue ribbon and wants to make sure that she has a pair of blue ribbons, how many more ribbons does Sarah need to select? Explain your answer.

_____

5. If Sarah pulled 1 yellow ribbon and wants to make sure that she has a pair of yellow ribbons, how many more ribbons does Sarah need to select?

_____

6. If Sarah first pulled a pink ribbon and wants to make sure that she has a pair of pink ribbons, how many more ribbons does Sarah need to select? Why is this less than first pulling out yellow or blue?

_____

© Pearson Education, Inc. 4

State Predictions

John and Jessica are assigned to collect data for a school project. They need to find out which of 4 U.S. states the students would like to learn more about: Florida, California, Oregon, or Colorado.

It is impossible to ask all of the 500 students at their school, so they decided to collect some sample data.

- John surveyed 10 students: 7 chose California and 3 chose Florida.

- Jessica surveyed 50 students: 25 chose California, 10 chose Florida, 10 chose Oregon, and 5 chose Colorado.

1. Using John's data, predict the number of students who would choose to know more about each state.

   _____

   _____

2. Using Jessica's data, predict the number of students who would choose to know more about each state.

   _____

   _____

3. Which survey do you think is a more accurate prediction of the students' choices? Why?

   _____

   _____

4. What things might influence the predictions when taking a sample?

   _____

   _____

© Pearson Education, Inc. 4

A Graph Tells Stories

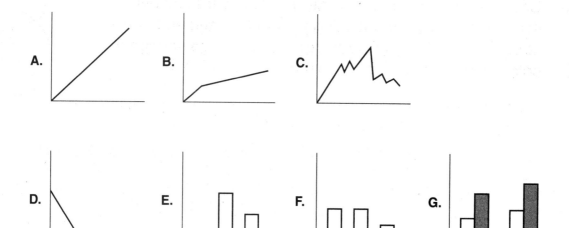

A.   B.   C.

D.   E.   F.   G.

The graphs have no labels on them, but you should be able to identify them from the type of information each contains. Write the letter of the correct graph in the space provided.

1. Jason's income from his dog-walking service rose quickly as he gained new customers, and then rose more slowly. _____

2. This year's school store and cafeteria both showed an increase in profits this year over last year. _____

3. The biking club noticed that the rate of speed went down by 2 mi an hour for every mile they biked. _____

4. Janet spends an equal time reading and playing sports but less time watching television. _____

5. The value of Mark's stock rose sharply at first and then fell and rose several times. _____

6. Most students preferred to do their homework after dinner, some right after school, and almost none in the morning. _____

7. Santi's plant experiment showed a steady growth of 2 cm a week. _____

© Pearson Education, Inc. 4

Name_____

Coloring Maps

1. Use a pencil to draw a squiggly line. Cross the line over itself repeatedly, without lifting your pencil, and end at the starting point. Be sure your segments are large enough to color. Here is an example of what it might look like.

2. Make a prediction. If you use four colors, can you color the various segments of your squiggly design so that no two adjacent segments are the same color?

_____

3. Color your squiggly design using four colors.

4. If you use three colors, can you color the various segments of your squiggly design so that no two adjacent segments are the same color?

_____

5. Here is a map of the island of Oldman. Color the waters surrounding the island blue. Color the rest using no more than four other colors. (Remember no colors should touch.)

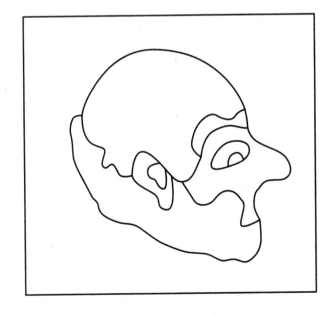

© Pearson Education, Inc. 4